You Can Only Drink But So Much Whine

Is Your Job Driving You To Drink?

T. Armstrong Dobson

Armstrong Assets
New Jersey

This publication is designed to entertain and provide suggestions to consider regarding the subject matter covered by the publisher and author. It is sold with the understanding that neither the publisher nor author is engaging in rendering professional advice or services of any kind and should not be held liable to such.

Printed in the United States of America
First Printing: August 2011

Library of Congress Cataloging in Publication Data:

Dobson, T. Armstrong
You Can Only Drink but So Much Whine: Is Your Job Driving you to Drink / T. Armstrong Dobson.

ISBN-13: 978-0-615-50381-3

Library of Congress Control Number: 2011912196

Dedicated to my father, the late William (Blake) L. Armstrong. A joyous, hilarious, and caring man who taught me the word " retirement" at a very early age and instructed me as I got older to get a "real job".

Daddy, may you rest in peace knowing that your laughter and personality continues to live strong in the memories of everyone that was blessed to have known you.

XOXO,
Jug

ACKNOWLEDGMENTS

I have always believed in miracles. However, the Lord continues to give me confirmation of his miracles on a daily basis. The completion of this book is one of the many miracles that I have been blessed to experience. Through this memorable process, I received divine assistance and support from many. I am so grateful for my family, friends, and former co-workers who have all given me many reasons and experiences to write this book.

I would like to thank the So Much Whine Movement which includes all my friends, relatives, former co-workers, my Fab 5, church members, association /club members, etc. All of you have allowed me to learn through your work experiences while providing encouragement during my own work experiences. To all of you, I sincerely appreciate your laughter, your tears, your stories, your trust, and your continuing support.

I would like to recognize my book creation team. Thank you, Karen O. for being the first cheerleader of the book while transforming my handwritten "chicken scratch" notes into the beginning of the first electronic manuscript. Thank you Matt for turning my words and vision into a funny and customized comic strip. Thank you Pete Pete for taking the time to build such a great "So Much Whine" website in conjunction of doing your own nine to five. Thank you Miss Pearl for having the patience and brilliance to edit my book with laughter and joy while constantly reminding me that it is "my book".

I want to acknowledge my close family who has always been there to tell me what I need to hear even if it is not what I want to hear. Thank you Sonya B. for all the great ideas and the daily encouragement calls to check on both my book progress and my energy in the midst of your own exciting adventure. Thank you Wynton for believing in me enough to make a large book purchase prior to the first release. Thank you to my sister LaWann for being my faithful blog reader and for your enduring term "Hey Lady, you can do it". Thank you to Nell, my mother, who has always listened to much whine while supporting and encouraging me with her great advice to "pray about it". Thank you to my wonderful and brilliant son, Dre' who always has a "you go mama" when I need it the most. Thank you to my husband Cedric, the consistent calm through every storm who has supported my ideas (good or bad) with unwavering love for over 20 years- you are my friend, spiritual brother, lover, and soul mate.

Most importantly, I thank God for the continuous grace and mercy that will continue to bless, protect and guide me throughout this journey called Life.

Thanks again to everyone and remember that we are all too blessed to have "So Much Whine!!!"

ABOUT THIS BOOK

How often have we found ourselves in conversations whining about the different dramas on the job?

Due to the frequency and depressive nature of these conversations, I often found myself desiring a glass of wine to endure the numerous work complaints of friends, family, and colleagues. One day I decided that enough was enough and I no longer wanted to participate in the daily whine nor the nightly wine that was being caused by a negative and dramatic workplace. Instead, I chose to be a part of the solution for improved workplace environments.

The first step in my quest for an improved workplace environment is to disclose the unwritten and unofficial taboos and behaviors that significantly impact the culture of our corporate world. I was also compelled to put certain things out in the open and on the table that will encourage employees and employers to consistently evaluate their morals, values, and sanity.

This book will bring to light some of the experiences that I have encountered as both an employee within multiple corporate roles and, most importantly, as a Human Resources Professional.

Employees at every level of the corporate ladder will directly or indirectly relate to the workplace experiences that are shared within these pages. Therefore, the entire workforce will benefit from this book by allowing it to assist them in explaining, resolving, applying, or avoiding some of the behaviors that I will discuss. This information will pose as a survival manual to someone who is newly entering the workforce, and serve as a sanity check for those currently in the workplace. It is also humorous enough to entertain the retiree who remembers the corporate environment all too well.

After reading this book, you will be reassured and relieved to have evidence to support the fact that today's workplace will drive you to drink (*if you let it*).

HOW TO USE THIS BOOK

This book utilizes a pun by addressing the workplace "Whine" within the world of "Wine".

The Whine list:

This is a table of contents that includes a list of the titles for each discussion

The Whine Collection:

Each section begins with down to earth discussions that are communicated in an "over a glass of wine" perspective and point of view. Hence, "The Whine!"

Pass the Whine:

This is a cartoon that illustrates the topic of each discussion. It will prove to be both humorous and thought provoking.

The Vineyard View:

This section provides opinions, facts, and possible solutions from the wisdom of a HR professional and Corporate Culture Coach.

Grapes of Wisdom:

This section is small tokens of advice from the author to enhance your life both inside and outside of the workplace. The section entitled "Vinetage Harvest" is a summary of all the Grapes of Wisdom.

The Whine Cellar:

This section includes references, additional readings, and popular sayings or word's from the Author's personal dictionary. It is great information to store in the cellar of your mind for future use.

The Whine List

Who's the Fool?

At some point in everyone's career, there comes a time when you feel as though you are above and beyond the point of being fooled. Although many think that they have seen it all and have heard it all, I don't think that anyone can totally avoid ever being the fool. It is easier to avoid becoming the fool when you have your guard up against cheesy sales people, criminals, pranksters, and evil dwellers. However, it is much easier to be caught off guard within your workplace.

Unfortunately, there are more political races being run within the workplace at any given time than there are outside the workplace. You never know who is saying what or doing what as a favor or trade negotiation for someone else to do or say whatever is desired or requested from another. It gets as complex as it sounds, but it goes on daily in the workplace and is somewhat considered "the corporate way".

There used to be some safety found in just keeping your head down and doing your job. However, times have changed due to the new "lean way" corporations are doing business which leaves no space for anyone to hide in the workplace. Since you have fewer people doing more tasks, everyone at some point is required to be "front and center" as it pertains to their sole responsibilities.

I realize that I should offer some advice as to how to protect yourself against the claws of corporate politics, but the best advice is to be aware that at any time and for any reason, you could be pulled into a political scheme at work. It will cause you to go through some unbelievable, face smiling/back stabbing, crackernacker bull without any fault of your own. You could simply be in the wrong place at the right time. So just take comfort in knowing that there is no exception to the rule… We must all someday play the fool.

pass the whine

pass the whine (cont'd)

pass the whine (cont'd)

pass the whine (cont'd)

Harry, there you go again trying to be the star individual contributor. "Team player" Harry – focus on being a "team player.

VINEYARD VIEW

There is a fine line between being a team player and being taken advantage of by team members. It is also important that clear expectations are communicated during performance evaluations. It should be confirmed that you and your manager have similar thoughts regarding actions that will indicate improvement in a developmental area. Therefore, you should ask for specific examples that would signify improvement. Or you should provide specific examples of what you could do to improve so that you gain agreement in advance of your actions.

Grapes of Wisdom

Hard work on your part does not necessarily equate to good work in the eyes of the evaluators who have their own expectations of what "good" looks like.

To Cc or Bcc?
This is the Question.

W hat is the message that we are sending when we copy or blind copy someone on an e-mail at work? When I receive a Cc (Carbon Copy) message, I think the sender would like me to assume one of the following:

1. They don't really know if they should be sending the e-mail to me since I was placed in the Cc section vs. the "To" section….. So, it is a "just in case" e-mail.

2. They want to be sure that I was aware of the information, and they also want the main recipient to be aware that they are informing me.

3. They want me to feel included, so they involved me out of pure courtesy, even if the information is irrelevant to me or does not require me to take any action.

On the occasions when I am included in the Bcc (Blind Carbon Copy) section on an e-mail, I think the sender is telling me the following:

1. They want me to see how courageous they are being by sending the e-mail to the recipient, although they are too much of a coward to openly Cc me on the message.

2.   They want me to see the message as documentation of proof in the future *(However, they should really be keeping their own CYA file)*.

3.   They want me to know what is really going on, although I should act as if I do not know. I should also not disclose who made me aware of the information.

What occurred to make it necessary to expand the simple "To" and "From" labels of an e-mail message? You should be sending the e-mail directly to me or probably not sending it to me at all. I also would like to know why Bcc was ever created to encourage cowardly or conniving behavior at work. The number of e-mails that we get daily at work would decrease greatly if people did not have the option to Cc or Bcc other people on the message.

The next time you send an e-mail and find yourself wondering if it is really necessary to include anyone else on the message along with your main recipients be sure to determine your motive. This will provide you with an answer for…"To Cc or Bcc?" ... *Since that is the question.*

pass the whine

pass the whine (Cont'd)

pass the whine (Cont'd)

VINEYARD VIEW

It is easy to get lazy and copy the entire world on an email without giving thought to who really needs the information. There is also a tendency to play "better safe than sorry". When the wrong decision is made to blind copy (BCC) or carbon copy (CC) different individuals, a large amount of the time is wasted shifting through unnecessary e-mails. In addition, much personal time is wasted reading e-mails on PDA devices just to keep up with them all.

If you would like to decrease unnecessary e-mails, it is totally acceptable to ask someone to exclude you from their distribution list regarding topics that you do not need to monitor closely. You can communicate that you would be satisfied with an e-mail on the final results or solutions on particular projects/ issues. If you are copied on an e-mail after a request to be excluded, it demonstrates a lack of respect that justifies the option of immediate deletion.

Grapes of Wisdom

A disregarded request for e-mail exclusion justifies immediate e-mail execution. Take control of your inbox.

Corporate Pimps

I'm sure this title has confused you immediately since most people would not think that the word "corporate" and "Pimps" belong in the same sentence. Well, I can reassure you that pimping does occur in the workplace every day. I have heard of many stories where leaders have provided unearned, unjustified, and undeserved gifts, opportunities, or fringe benefits to selected employees. Most of the recipients of these perks or incentives eagerly accept the so called "gifts" before identifying "the strings" that are attached to them. The strings are not shown until it is time to repay the favor in some way.

This strategy is typically used by incompetent leaders and/or leaders who need to create allies to cover bad behavior that is unacceptable in leadership roles (i.e. sexual harassment, hostile treatment, and noncompliant actions). Unfortunately, the "pimps" in the process will usually have the power and money to pull off these types of actions confidentially with ease. The gifts can be as small as additional days off, special office space, event tickets, etc. The gifts may be as large as promotions, company leased cars, expensive items, large cash amounts, rent payments, and even homes (I must say this last one is rare and it even surprised me, but yes it did occur!).

So if you are being pimped and are under the illusion that good fortunes have just fell into your lap without effort on your part or without any expectations, just be aware and prepared for the "big pay day". Payback can typically be described as performing some form of unethical act or being a willing scapegoat to protect the Pimp's job or reputation.

Unfortunately, if you decide not to cooperate with the payback terms, it could negatively affect your current role and possibly your employment with the company.

The easiest way to get out of this type of relationship is to stop accepting the gifts. I know it will be hard at first to let go of something that is not currently causing you any harm. However you must trust me when I say, "These situations will always end with the termination of one or both players". The game is always risky and the recipients are usually the only ones in the dark. Corporate pimping frequently occurs and many choose to do it. Crooked leaders are fully aware that..."Pimping *IS* Easy".

pass the whine

pass the whine (cont'd)

pass the whine (cont'd)

pass the whine (cont'd)

VINEYARD VIEW

At times, employees may be put in awkward positions by their superiors. However, it is important that employees are aware of state and federal laws that protect the employee. In "this for that" situations, Quid Quo Pro states that it is unlawful for anyone in a position higher than your own to offer you the choice of unethical behavior as an option over losing your job, position, projects, office space, etc.

Unfortunately, some situations are easier to prove than others. Simply communicating your knowledge of this law should decrease, if not deter, this type of treatment from affecting you. This is especially true if you refrain from accepting those "special gifts".

Grapes of Wisdom

Much is expected from those who have gained a great deal, but anything can be expected from those who have gained it unethically.

On to the Next One

The mind is a powerful organ. It is amazing how our thoughts can change our perception of things to the point that we experience a new situation in the midst of an old situation that hasn't changed. A perfect example of this theory is employees that know they will be leaving a company soon for a better opportunity. These employees seem to have recovered from having the "lip-out, moping, complaining (while under major stress and frustration) in an overnight timeframe. They have new energy as they smile and skip around the office singing "Don't worry, be happy". I love observing these situations while others are trying to discover what is different about the transformed employees.

I often figure out the reason for the transformation when someone is about to leave the company. These individuals have this "I don't care; you just wait until I am gone" look on their faces. My guess is often confirmed when I get a call from a vendor to verify their employment, but I usually keep these types of calls to myself. Why should I mess-up someone's countdown experience unnecessarily by spilling the beans? I think a company has waited too late to attempt to retain an employee that is already on the way out of the door.

So if you are blessed enough to find a better opportunity, good for you. Hold your head up high and keep a big smile during the last days of chaos until 5, 4, 3, 2, 1 ...YOU'RE GONE!!!)

pass the whine

pass the whine (cont'd)

VINEYARD VIEW:

It is always an exciting feeling to accept a new position. Employees should be sure to check the company's reference policy prior to exiting to ensure that your current company only provides your start and end date as reference information. There are not too many companies willing to offer any additional information in order to avoid accusations of slander from former employees. Employees should also strategize the exit date to coincide with a new company start date or any time off they want to have in between jobs.

Some people decide to use their vacation time to exit the company prior to the end of their two week notice, although most companies pay out cash for earned and unused vacation time in your last paycheck. Therefore, weigh your options on having the time off or the dollars. Since bad remarks travel fast, if you are staying in a certain field or industry, you may want to leave with a good reputation with all commitments completed or transitioned to someone else.

.

Grapes of Wisdom

A job, is a job, is a job. People, projects, and pay may change, but the definition remains the same – "you work, they pay, at first, you stay, until one day, you're on your way."

Who Gets the "Gold Star"?

The workplace was designed to allow mature adults to accomplish various assigned tasks in a healthy, respectful environment for a predetermined agreed upon amount of money.

OK. If this is true and it is just that simple, why do I spend countless hours listening to bickering adults who are not communicating effectively due to the lack of respect that they have for the workplace, one another, and themselves? There are many alternative occupations that I could have chosen outside of HR if I wanted to constantly play the detective, lawyer, referee, judge, or police.

It is insane how petty, immature, disrespectful, and selfish some employees behave at work. I often wonder if this type of behavior is carried out at work because it is tolerated in these individuals' homes. Also, it may be thought by some that victims at work will ignore or overlook this immature behavior because they do not want to deal with it. Well, I can surely understand individuals not wanting to deal with this kind of behavior. However, there are times that you are forced to deal with it (like me).

It takes so much energy to attempt to explain to "misbehaving employees" that their actions and words are unsatisfactory for the workplace. In addition, respectful behavior is hard to enforce if no laws or policies are being broken along the way. There is rarely a welcome in the workplace for a "Mother Theresa" moment or a "Dr. King" cry for unity. Besides, "Don't be a jerk" is left out of most employee handbooks.

Unfortunately, the nasty acting people at work get what they want when they want it as well as acknowledgement. I believe employees should be evaluated on how they get assignments accomplished vs., rewarding "by any means necessary" successes.

Someone must put a stop to the "cut throat" corporate mentality. It is up to all of us to "check" the behavior of each other and only award the "Gold Stars" to the well behaved boys and girls.

pass the whine

pass the whine (Cont'd)

VINEYARD VIEW:

Work should be a safe environment. Inappropriate language and disrespectful acts can create harassing or hostile environments. It is appropriate for employees to respectfully address anyone that is causing them discomfort at work due to their words or actions.

If an unsuccessful attempt has been made to end disrespectful words or inappropriate actions of a co-worker, employees should make a formal complaint of either harassment or a hostile work environment with their supervisor and/or Human Resources. It is important for you to have your complaint documented to support any further occurrences regarding the complaint.

Grapes of Wisdom

The acts of jerks and jackasses are not symptoms of a non-controllable disease, but their acts remain voluntary, selective, and are totally based on past responses/consequences from their targets. They will do unto you as you allow them to do.

Highly Contagious

Most people are cautious when it comes to protecting themselves from contagious illnesses. Unfortunately, employees are sometimes unaware of other very contagious issues in the workplace such as laziness, complacency, and half "A_ _" doing things. I see companies take valuable dollars and time to hire a high performer into a group of slackers. The thought process is that the new talent will assist in motivating the rest of the group. However, if radical changes and new expectations are not set at a high level, the high performer will be forced to constantly beg and pull for actions from fellow coworkers while being labeled as the "trouble maker" or "pain in the behind" of the group.

At some point, the high performer will become exhausted and give-up just to fit in. Ironically, the performance of the new employee to the group will not be negatively evaluated since even the lowest level of the top performer will still outdo the performance of the slackers. However, a long period of time in this type of environment will cause the high performer's achievement meter to be calibrated to a lower standard.

Once the high performer has an opportunity to move to a higher performing work team, he/she will suffer from the "slacker sniffles," "bad performer blues", or catch a case of the "crazy cough". These affected high performers will have to struggle to strengthen their performance muscles back to normal. So if you are the "A" student in a group of flunkies, I suggest you "get out" fast since there's no vaccine for whatever you might catch!!!

pass the whine

pass the whine (cont'd)

VINEYARD VIEW

Organizations are constantly trying to improve their business by becoming more competitive, earning higher profits and by hiring, developing, and retaining top talent. It is always important to interview with team members to gage the competency level and work ethics of your potential team. However, this may not always be achievable, especially if you are being transferred to a new team due to a re-organization vs. a new role that requires an external or internal interviewing process.

For those who are not fortunate to have an opportunity for a team preview, you must work by your own work standards, even if it means blowing the whistle and becoming a pain to slackers. Your end of the year performance review will be based on your results and not the participation or non-cooperation of co-workers.

Grapes of Wisdom

Avoid groups where you are the greatest contributor, the most knowledgeable, or the most competent. Either you are able to learn or grow from others, or you slowly decline while attempting to teach and grow yourself.

Square Peg, Round Hole

The large percentage of people who are unhappy with their jobs is constantly being analyzed and questioned. I know there are issues with bosses and coworkers that may contribute to some of this unhappiness. However, there are also those individuals who feel as though they are spending 8-10 hours a day and 5-6 days a week doing jobs that contradict who they are naturally. I understand that some roles are accepted to aid in developmental areas. However, I also believe that most people who aim to work on true weaknesses will only end up with strengthened weaknesses.

After years of watching employees struggle in misfit roles, I believe time is better used when people choose to strengthen average or strong areas into becoming stronger. It is less stressful and more rewarding to acknowledge your authentic self. Life is too short and going to work takes up a large percentage of your daily life. Therefore, you should make the decision to be victorious at "doing you"…and leave the round holes for the round pegs

pass the whine

VINEYARD VIEW

There are a variety of assessments for employees to take to understand the following: work type enjoyed; individual work strengths; low interest areas; or work areas that lack ability.

These assessments will assist employees in determining if they dislike their job due to the lack of interest, lack of skill, or both. Some employees will also discover that they do not desire or have interest for their role although they perform well in it. Others will discover that they need to fine tune raw talent and develop that talent to become successful in a role that they truly desire, although initially they may not be totally efficient in the role.

Grapes of Wisdom

A bad day of being who you are will yield better results than a good day of you attempting to be who you are not.

What Came First, the Drama or the Job?

Life is short. We spend a large amount of our lives at work. I'm probably not being realistic by thinking that everyone should enjoy their job 100%. However, I do feel that it is unhealthy for people to be at a job that makes them emotionally, mentally, and physically ill. More than ever, the news is filled with stories of frustrated employees committing suicide, holding co-workers hostage, or angry employees who go "postal" or ballistic and shoot up their workplace....All due to unhappiness with their work or the loss of a job.

As a HR professional, I often wonder if corporations are hiring crazy people or if they are creating them. I often try to identify people who are successful and thriving in the corporate setting without sacrificing their values and desires within their personal life. There is a small percentage of these individuals who have found the balance of a successful work life with a satisfying and well-rounded personal life.

I realize that we go to work to do a job. However, my definition of a job is "the primary activity in your life that you do to earn money". This definition doesn't say anything about a job needing to be the most stressful, difficult part of your day. Nor does it indicate that a job is a substitute for a fulfilling life with cherished family and friends. The definition simply states that you get paid for a task that you do.

With all the issues at work, there must be another legal and less stressful way to earn a living. We all have the option to be employees *(which means you will have at least one boss)* or entrepreneurs *(which*

The Whine Collection 7: What Came Frist, the Drama or the Job?

33

often means that you will have multiple bosses in the form of clients and customers). Regardless of which path you choose, it really comes down to two choices. 1) Go to work, get paid, and work at balancing the drama OR 2) Don't work, don't get paid, and create drama. Drama will exist if you have a job, and it will surely exist if you don't. This question remains unanswered for many. Do we bring our drama to the job or is the job the source of our drama?

pass the whine

pass the whine (Cont'd)

The Whine Collection 7: What Came Frist, the Drama or the Job?

35

pass the whine (Cont'd)

pass the whine (Cont'd)

VINEYARD VIEW

Stress is often the main issue behind many workplace problems. The stress may come from our workload, management issues, co-worker relationships, health problems, financial worries, lay-offs, or family issues. Many organizations offer employee assistance (EAP) programs to assist employees with stress. However, many employees do not use the EAP benefits.

Some organizations have more innovative ways for employees to manage stress such as an on-site masseuse, napping rooms, exercise facilities, corporate parks, etc. Companies are on the bandwagon to assist employees with managing stress to decrease the corporation's medical insurance cost, to increase employees' work productivity and, of course, to prevent any possible "postal" events at the workplace. Stress is not avoidable, but employees can take control of how they handle stress by taking advantage of stress management resources.

Grapes of Wisdom

Stress is a self-induced internal reaction that will follow you
wherever you go.

All Dressed-up with NOWHERE to Go...

Many companies take pride in advertising that they "promote from within". Some companies also have excellent development programs to provide their employees with the resources to prepare them for the next level. Unfortunately, the process to move up in an organization is more complex than the expectations of working hard, gaining new skills, or passing assessments. Politics also play a major role in the internal promotion process.

It only takes one negative perception or comment from the appropriate level to smash your promotion possibilities. Importance is usually placed on the messenger instead of the accuracy of the information *(so truth has no value to receivers who get a so-called "heads-up" from a high level)*. Keep in mind, most high performers who show interest in moving up in the company will typically be granted an interview *(either formally or informally)*. This strategy shows the employees that they are viewed as valuable while preventing them from leaving the organization *(even if there is no intention of promoting them)*.

I think it is a shame to have an employee who is anticipating a bona-fide interview to go through the motions of preparation to meet with a group of leaders who are all aware that a different hire has already been identified for the role prior to scheduling the meeting. I want you to be aware of this type of corporate act, although there isn't much you can do to identify it when it is occurring (some *leaders have an expertise with deception in this area*).

38

Even if you don't get the initial promotion, remember that you must always strive to develop your skills or abilities because it could be for either an internal or external move to the next level...... You never know when you will actually have the opportunity to be all dressed-up with SOMEWHERE to go.

pass the whine

pass the whine (Cont'd)

pass the whine (Cont'd)

VINEYARD VIEW

Development of the current work staff is important to many organizations. Unfortunately, it is sometimes difficult to manage the desires of employees with the needs of the company business without a structured process to address internal interest in company job openings. This process should provide clarity for employees while ensuring fair and consistent treatment of all internal candidates. However, if you are not fortunate enough to have such a process, it is necessary to take the process into your own hands.

The first step is to identify the role you are interested in pursuing. Next, you should identify the qualifications of the desired role through research and attendance in informal information sessions with someone who is currently in the role. You should also identify a leadership mentor who will be able to be your advocate and provide professional instructions on addressing the talents and skills that you need to sharpen or gain to qualify for the desired role.

As you are developing for the role, either you or your advocate should communicate your interest in the desired role to the potential leader or team. A proper introduction will determine if they will take you seriously, regardless of your future development or achievements, to qualify for a desired opening on their team.

Either way, the good news is that you will have gained a mentor/coach, additional development skills, and the decision of if you should or should not waste time in an internal interview when an opening is finally available.

Grapes of Wisdom

Goals that are truly important to you should create self-motivation that will out-last the motivation from others

C.Y.A

It is a difficult task to balance our own work characteristics with the work characteristics of coworkers. The workplace is filled with employees who have different types of work ethic (some employees work hard, some work just enough, and others try not to work at all). There are also different proficiencies of time management ("in a minute" may mean seconds for some, hours for some, and days for others). The art of mastering various expectations is also difficult (since expectations may range from "I thought that was my responsibility", to "I thought you were going to do that," to "Let's just skip that action step this time".)

Although balancing all of these differences can be very stressful and complex, we need others within the workplace to ensure that our own tasks/projects are completed successfully and on time. Therefore, we must handle and manage these differences since we cannot avoid them.

Throughout my career, I have tried many strategies to adjust to the many differences. My goal would be to refrain from turning into one of those "got to have it this way, at this time, on this day, or I'm going to the boss" type of coworker. However, there have been situations when the "please understand my timeline and expectations" tactic did not work.

When you find yourself in similar situations where fellow coworkers are mistaking your kindness as an overkill of patience and understanding, there are only a few things that you can do to keep your cool while ensuring that you are not held accountable for the inefficiencies of others.

You should C.Y.A...
- Change Your Attitude
- Call Your Allies
- Constrain Yelling Aloud
- Confirm Yesterday's Agreements
- Challenge "Yes" Answers

Regardless of which C.Y.A you choose, I saved the most important, most popular, truest, and most utilized C.Y. A. for last. Even if you forget all the others, Cover Your As…sets! (*to be more professionally correct*)

pass the whine

pass the whine (Cont'd)

pass the whine (Cont'd)

pass the whine (Cont'd)

VINEYARD VIEW

The culture of a workplace, a particular industry, and the level of accountability will dictate the degree of CYA needed by an employee to cover or prevent them from being blamed for future issues.

The best HR advice that I can provide on this topic is to strive to communicate in a clear and concise matter. It is important to shy away from assumptions, sarcasm, or exaggerations when you communicate about work in the workplace. In addition, you should keep documentation on certain topics that will serve as protection if your actions are ever questioned in the future. It is smart to keep this information in two forms or locations since computers are known to crash.

Grapes of Wisdom

The selective memory of others can easily translate into an opportunity to guess your past actions and responses for their benefit; only evidence from you provides true confirmation.

Going Once, Going Twice...SOLD!

All of us work for companies that are selling something. Depending on the industry, the company may sell tangible goods or provide a type of service. In addition, all employees are typically selling concepts and solutions. In the midst of all the above selling processes, there is also a less visible transaction occurring daily. The individuals involved in this particular transaction are either oblivious or ashamed of its occurrence. It is rarely planned and it usually happens during a fork in the road that causes them to either choose option 1: whatever is honorable or option 2: whatever will cover their butt and ultimately throw someone else under the bus.

There are times when employees will choose the first option. Although the first option may cause foreseen drama, it will immediately abort the sales transaction. The second option may also be chosen. If selected, the second option ends the transaction and the sale of the person's soul is complete.

Unfortunately, once employees get over the fact that they have completed the unpopular sale of their soul, they will usually attend these sales events numerous times in their career. These individuals are easy to spot because they are known for inconsistencies, selective memory, and bold faced lies. These individuals are called "sell outs". Regardless of the situation, if it puts a "sell out" in the hot seat for any length of time, a "FOR SALE" sign appears on their forehead and they are "SOLD" to the highest bidder.

pass the whine

pass the whine (Cont'd)

pass the whine (Cont'd)

VINEYARD VIEW

The workplace is highly competitive. However, there are times to shine as individual competitors and times to ensure that you are being a team player. Also, there

are times for employees to push back on unrealistic deadlines. Pushback is professional, fact-based conversations that communicate the reason more time is needed, consequences of the unrealistic time line, and the lack of quality that is associated with the suggested deadline.

It should always be communicated well in advance that deadlines may not be met to allow the leaders and others to adjust their work and their expectations prior to the initial deadline date.

Grapes of Wisdom

1. The true meaning of team is Together Execute Actions Masterfully.

2. Expectations control the emotional responses to unmet deadlines.

On the Ledge

OMG, this world is full of drama! Believe it or not, there are Drama Kings and Queens within the workplace as well. Every small situation or incident becomes a theatrical event. Something is always wrong. Everything is always critical or urgent. These employees never have a positive report about anything. They mope around the office with an expression that reads, "If you say anything to me, I will pass out because I am far too busy to take one more command."

These people are always out sick. They also are great record keepers of their FLMA rights and their eligibility for short or long term disability. In an effort to avoid work, they use short or long term disability to protect their jobs. Therefore, they get the process started by convincing a doctor and others that they are suicidal and negatively affected by their job.

As a HR professional, I think it is unacceptable for a company to allow an employee to be pushed to this state of mind. Employees should be able to work in a stable environment that is healthy for both their bodies and their minds. However, since I have been round the block and have both intellect and street smarts, I know that all people who are out on the ledge are not created equal.

So, allow me to excuse the employees who are legitimately stressed out by their job. To these employees, I give my deepest condolences. Now, for the slackers who are avoiding work, cheating the system, and looking for sympathy: If I have just described you, and you are pretending to be on the ledge, just know that you are a pain to all HR professionals, and we all have one word for you…JUMP!

pass the whine

pass the whine (Cont'd)

VINEYARD VIEW

There are laws in place to protect the job of employees who need to take care of their health and the heath of immediate family members. The government ensures that these laws are followed by implementing the Family Medical Leave Act. It is great protection for those who need it. On the other hand, there are some employees that abuse the system with false illnesses and fabricated paperwork.

Unfortunately, the false cases are usually hard to confirm since the cases are supported by a licensed physician who has been deceived or who has volunteered to play along. In addition, mental illnesses are easily exaggerated without required tests for diagnosis. These types of fraudulent incidences are illegal and risk the job of both the employee and the physician. Nevertheless, there are individuals that have decided that this type of action is worth avoiding work or an anticipated termination.

Grapes of Wisdom

Karma has a sense of humor, so whatever you fake to do may eventually come true.

Go Get Em'

It has been said that the second biggest fear next to dying is public speaking. Many people go through major anxiety when it comes to giving presentations. Fortunately, I do not share this level of anxiety when I speak in public, but I do get nervous or become very concerned when I do not follow the basic three rules of public speaking: 1) know your information, 2) be familiar with your audience and their expectations of you, and 3) be aware of pitfalls/areas of concern ahead of time.

Once you satisfy the three basic rules, you can use your energy to connect with your audience. It is difficult to be at ease when are trying to skate through information that you do not know while praying that no one will have a question. It is also hard to speak to a group and add value if you are not aware of their concerns or relevance to your topic.

Lastly, it is much easier to handle an area of concern or to address a difficult question if you have prepared for this before the presentation. This preparation will prevent you from bombing under pressure. It will also prevent haters from taking you down rabbit holes off your planned path because you were caught off guard.

Once you adhere to the 3 basic rules and successfully connect with your audience, you will experience the true joy of public speaking. Your audience will feel that you were confident, valuable, and resourceful. Just remember – when you know your stuff, know your audience, and have a clear path around the possible land mines, you can nail your presentation.

pass the whine

passs the whine (cont'd)

passs the whine (cont'd)

VINEYARD VIEW

Public speaking in the work environment can sometimes be a difficult task. Many companies will reimburse their employees who want to take courses or workshops to sharpen their presentation skills, especially when presenting is a function of their job. Some larger organizations or metro cities have toastmaster clubs that will assist employees to improve their comfort and proficiency level in public speaking and presenting.

One of the biggest fears of public speaking is to have a heckler in the audience. Unfortunately, hecklers in the work environment disguise themselves as well-meaning individuals that have questions throughout your presentation. These corporate hecklers will attempt to test your competency level of the topic, your patience, and your ability to focus with frequent interruptions.

Although this is a difficult situation to solve in front of an audience, it is not only doable, but acceptable. If you do not have the privilege to politely ask the known trouble makers to behave or to hold their questions for a personal sidebar, you may, while in front of an audience, ask the person to refrain from any additional questions and allow you to arrange a private meeting for them at another time to avoid prolonging the presentation. Then you can soften this response by thanking them for such extreme interest in your topic.

The sole focus of delivering a good presentation should be on providing important information, facts, or statistics to your audience. An audience will give a presentation a good evaluation if the presenter was understood, connected well, and provided valuable information.

Grapes of Wisdom

Be careful of how you use the tongue. Proven to be the strongest muscle in the body, it can pick up or tear down the spirits of an entire audience at the same time.

Silently Speaking

People who have jobs that are hectic, stressful, and fast paced on a daily basis have an appreciation for silence at work. Many view the silence as a pleasant opportunity to catch up on work assignments. There are others who are made uneasy by the silence. These individuals view the silence timeframe as torture because they expect the flood gates to open with additional work to make up for lost time. I must admit that a long abnormal silence in the workplace can be unnerving.

Although this is not an official theory, my theory is that abnormal silence at work is a sign of an unexpected lay off, acquisition, or major business decision. Leaders will usually put a hold on major decisions, projects, and budgets during these quiet but critical times. The instructions to reduce business actions will spiral down into the organization and show-up as slower and quieter work days.

Although this theory has been proven to be true on many occasions, I still choose to enjoy silence whenever possible at work. These prolonged and rare times should be used to relax, re-energize, and refocus. You could also use the time to get extra work done, but realize that you may be putting useless energy into finishing a project that may be cancelled or deemed unsatisfactory due to changing objectives.

Employees that are aware of this theory may choose to do extra work to decrease their odds of possibly being laid off (*Sorry, this type of decision has already been made before the silent period, so extra work will not save you at this point*).

Regardless of how you decide to use quiet time, you should keep your ears and eyes open. Leaders can sometimes be too quiet, which means they are probably up to something. Furthermore, an abnormal period of silence is usually the "calm before the storm".

pass the whine

pass the whine (cont'd)

pass the whine (cont'd)

VINEYARD VIEW

For various reasons, mainly the economy, many organizations must down size, re-organize, or undergo an acquisition. Unfortunately, these topics are kept highly confidential until the situation is completely planned or until it has occurred. However, there are actions that must be taken to save money or to reduce the level of risk to the anticipated business agreement.

It is always wise to be aware of unusual actions in the workplace. Being aware may allow you to prepared by identifying a new internal opportunity prior to a mass re-organization or allow adequate time to seek an opportunity externally prior to a mass lay-off. If asked, some heart-felt superiors may be able to tell you "what" you should do, even if they cannot disclose "why" you should do it.

Grapes of Wisdom

The calm before the storm may be your last chance to run.

AWOL

During a period of a new boss from outer space, your job will never be the same. At least once a month, you will seriously consider getting up from your desk and walking away from your job without ever looking back or providing a resignation.

It is a shame to let it get to this point, but we are all human with limitations. Nonetheless, it is important that we keep our work situations in perspective. We should ensure that we are not contributing to the chaos and that we have communicated our dissatisfaction. I realize that the current economy has everyone preaching the same…cliché "you should be grateful to have a job." I do believe that you should be grateful if you are blessed with a paycheck. On the other hand, a more realistic statement is "sometimes we do what we have to do even if it isn't what we want to do."

So, the next time you get the feeling to leave work and walk jobless into the sunset, know that you are not alone. Unfortunately for some, their mind and body are telling them to go, but their wallet is screaming... NO!

68

pass the whine

pass the whine

VINEYARD VIEW

Similar to going AWOL in the armed services, leaving a job without notice is frowned upon. However, there are no legal ramifications if a notice is not provided as long as there is not a breach of contract. Most people and companies believe a two week or more notice is mandatory, but most of the time it is not. On the contrary, there are laws to protect employees from sudden, unjustified, discriminatory, or mass lay-offs. Some of these include non at will states, and laws such as Title VII and the Warn Act. On the other side, employees are free to leave a non-contractual position at any time.

The results of leaving a company abruptly would probably decrease your chances for re-hire, and the co-worker gossip grapevine could possibly hurt your professional industry reputation. However, note during future employment verifications that most organizations will only provide your first/ last day, your most recent job title, your boss's name and, in some cases, your salary. Performance detailed references are often avoided by corporations to protect them from being accused of "slander".

Grapes of Wisdom

If you can no longer take the heat, first decide how hungry you are before leaving the kitchen.

Risky Business

It always starts innocently enough. "Do you want to grab some lunch?" "This was a rough day; let's go get a drink after work." "It's getting late, do you want to finish the final touches of the presentation over dinner?" It sometimes begins with conversations that are non- business related such as "What do you do for fun? "My husband/ wife/ boy or girlfriend has really pissed me off!" or "You are so easy to talk to, and I'm having a serious personal problem and want to get your advice". I am not saying that any of the above scenarios are unacceptable or inappropriate employee activities. What I am saying is that this is how "risky business" often starts before it jumps off.

Regardless of how it starts, risky business will also go to the next level unless one participant makes it very clear that the relationship has not or will not even be considered going beyond the relationship of a co-worker (*which just happens to be a decent person to speak to, trust, and laugh with every now and then*). The individuals that decide to take it beyond work are always identified easily. These individuals are always together, always e-mailing/instant messaging and finding excuses to be in the same meetings, groups, or projects.

Since the majority of the workforce are grown adults, it should not matter if they are looking for love in the wrong places. To clarify, these individuals are not always single. Infidelity is also a personal choice. The biggest problem with this bad decision is that it will eventually fall down. Someone will be found out by their spouse, or someone will get mad and call it quits. Unfortunately, the show must still go on at work.

Therefore, these people are stuck with the awkward and undesired run-ins at the office.

Although a failed corporate romance is always highly uncomfortable for the involved employees, the company couldn't care less. The company is only concerned when the relationship ends negatively where one participant files a sexual harassment case because: 1.) they got scared and changed their mind; 2.) someone decided to stay in his/her marriage; 3.) one party became angry about how the relationship ended. A sexual harassment claim is also used to allow the accuser to quickly snatch the title of victim to derail any further office gossip.

I have done a few investigations that have uncovered initial sexual consent, but a 90 degree turn suddenly occurred for whatever reason. Regardless, the company will support the accuser and do whatever is necessary to document that proper measures have been taken to protect and punish the appropriate parties.

Take my word for it--these types of situations have ended in court cases, job loss, divorces, demotions, and bitter backlashes. If you decide to find out the hard way and insist on giving the office relationship a "TRY," beware of the consequences of a corporate B-U-D-D-Y.

pass the whine

pass the whine (Cont'd)

pass the whine (Cont'd)

pass the whine (Cont'd)

VINEYARD VIEW

It is truly unrealistic to believe that relationships of all kinds will not develop in the workplace. Some people meet best friends, husbands, wives, future business partners, etc. on the job. The key is not necessarily to avoid all workplace relationships altogether. However, it is important to set standards for what is and is not acceptable for each employee. The best choice is to examine if the relationship can negatively affect work performance or work decisions. It should also be discussed how the end of the relationship will affect your job in the future.

It is totally acceptable to choose your current position or a potential relationship over one another. It totally depends on the associated risk and what is most important to each of you at the time. Please be aware that an important decision between two involved individuals in a workplace relationship may need to be made one day.

Grapes of Wisdom

All secret relationships are temporary since privacy or patience is guaranteed to run out at some point.

Far From The Truth

HR professionals receive a number of lies on numerous occasions. Although I have gotten used to the lies, I am still fascinated by the different techniques and strategies that are used in an attempt to deceive even the most brilliant individuals.

There are many clues to alert you when someone is not telling the truth. These clues have been tested and disclosed to the majority of the population. Therefore, people who lie are very careful not to show any of the following clues during an untruthful conversation.

· They don't blink frequently or look away from the person;

· They do not stutter or pause for too long;

· They refrain from quickly changing the subject and do not use too many Uhhs and Ahhhs;

· They maintain stable movements with both their hands and their feet;

· They avoid coughing and frequently clearing their throat.

So if you were looking for any of the above clues to determine when someone is lying to you at work, you should be aware that the game has changed within the corporate walls. Co-workers will skillfully look you in your face, not show any of the typical signs of deceit, and tell you a "boldfaced" lie. I have experienced so many untruthful tales that I have picked up on a new set of clues that will alert you to corporate lies.

My most recently discovered clues include the following:

· They speak very formally and assertively in the attempt to be viewed as confident and credible.

· They have plastered forced smiles that do not match their words, tone, or your reaction/response.

· They do an obsessive amount of dropping of a leader's name to try to prevent you from questioning their decision or judgment.

· Regardless of how inconvenient the situation may be, they insist on having the conversation face to face or by live phone call to avoid any document trail of the discussion.

· Before telling the lie, they attempt to butter you up by disclosing some information in confidence to demonstrate that they trust you so you should trust them.

There are probably many more clues and the list of clues grows larger each day. You should remember that the workplace is full of talented individuals and some of these individuals have a talent of creating a professional, well-thought out, so very convincing LIE! This is a fact that you CAN believe.

pass the whine

pass the whine (Cont'd)

VINEYARD VIEW

Similar to any situation in a non-work environment, people in a work place environment either lie to manipulate or to protect. Unfortunately, work place lies may unnecessarily cause the organization to break labor, government, or industry policies/ laws. It is also common for people to discover workplace lies and not confront the deceiver. Instead, the person who discovered the lie will create a permanent stigma against the deceiver and will secretly share this information with others. This is especially true with HR or leadership since they do not want the deceitful employee to associate any future treatment from others with the discovered lie. Therefore, you never really know for sure if you are getting away with your lies since falsification is rarely disclosed unless it is the last alternative to saving the company from risk or another employee from termination.

Grapes of Wisdom

The "Truth" may cause brief discomfort, but it will ultimately provide relief. A clever "lie" causes false comfort and creates stress and strain.

Set It Off

There are many techniques used by leadership to distinguish the disposable employees from the next leaders. This evaluation is primitive to say the least.

It happens very quickly. At first, you consider yourself paranoid because you can sense that something isn't right. All of a sudden your boss is assigning you major projects without the proper resources or manpower to complete the tasks. You know that your boss is aware of the extensive workload that is currently on your plate. You also know that your boss is well aware of your lack of manpower since you were informed of the decrease in headcount. In the same breath, the boss told you that you would not be able to hire a replacement for the direct report that just left your team. Regardless of how or why your bosses would know about the circumstances that they are making your job very challenging, bosses are aware and it seems like they do not really care.

Some people see this extra workload as a punishment. However, being in HR, I can assure you that there are ways far less risky ways to punish an employee than to give them highly visible projects that they could muck up to put the business at jeopardy. Punishment is usually grunt work projects that will not negatively affect your boss or the company if you fail.

There is a better word to describe high performing workers who are getting high level projects dumped on them without the appropriate resources. I call this the "SET-UP". Yes, you are being set up to see if you are worthy of the next level.

84

It is hard for some leaders to determine your readiness without this test because they believe that prior to passing the test you may grow horns, delegate a great deal of work, and run a few folks under the bus. You may also resort to creative ways (*both unethical and immoral*) to come out victorious from the big load of crap that has strategically been dumped upon you.

You have already been viewed as the hard worker that will always deliver desired results (*This is the first qualifier for a Set-up*). Although the cut throat-- by any means necessary--crap on others characteristics have not been proven to always be used by successful leaders, it is essential that a potential leader possess these characteristics in case they are needed in the future to get the job done.

The individuals that are giving you the test will be OK if you pass the test and OK if you fail. If you pass the test, they will have found a new leader. If you fail the test, they will begin the process to look for a new leader.

If you are in the midst of a similar test, you must remember that the only way to keep your job once you are given the test is to pass the test. So, you must decide if you are leaving or staying with the company.

Personally, I am one who prefers to leave a company on my own accord.Therefore, I would suggest that you strategically work out a plan to succeed so you can prove that even during a SET-UP you can set it off.

Knowing how grueling this test can be, you will probably be exhausted and a little angry about the test. So while everyone is in the middle of celebrating your victory, you can quickly get over being set-up by putting your sights on a promotion or a new company and getting set ....to JET.

pass the whine

pass the whine (Cont'd)

VINEYARD VIEW

Employees should always remember that every organization is a business. Consequently, there is a consistent desire to grow and protect the business. Although workloads may not always be fair, the intention is to always get good work from competent people.

Unfortunately, the only way for overworked employees to get the attention of their leadership is to attempt to communicate the risk to the company that could exist from dropping certain tasks, not having appropriate resources to complete important projects, or the possibility of you moving on to a more realistic workload at another company. (*You should not "call wolf" if this possibility is unlikely since they may call your bluff.*)

The most important thing to note is that work is always given to the proven competent and dependable people regardless of how fair it may or may not be. It is never a punishment when it is work of importance. Punishments are often very identifiable to the victims and all of their co-workers. Overworked Set-up employees will need to decide if they desire the "one day reward," if the reward will be worth all the effort, or if the reward will show up before they are totally burnt out and unable to transition with ease to a new opportunity.

Grapes of Wisdom

Hard work is always rewarded even if the actual award is not always in plain view.

Hide N' Seek

How many times has someone at work claimed that he has been "trying to get in touch with you"? For some reason, I am immediately irritated by this simple comment. I guess my irritation stems from my awareness of how slackers have a habit of hiding on the job. The mere fact that someone has tried to find you implies that you are hard to get, you fail to communicate your whereabouts, or that you are a hiding slacker attempting to avoid any additional questions or responsibilities.

Although there are probably some people at work that make me wish I was invisible, I follow the proper corporate etiquette of leaving an "out of office message" or "all day meeting message" on my voicemail, e-mail, and information with the appropriate administrative assistant. Therefore, I am so puzzled when I hear anyone at work make a comment that draws the conclusion that someone at work is trying to FIND me. I typically respond to these types of comments with the following questions:

- Did you call my office? Did you leave a message?
- Did you call my cell phone? Did you leave a message?
- Did you send me an e-mail?
- Did you send me a postal letter?
- Did you attempt to visit my office?
- Or did you go out of your way to call or visit my home?

The way I see it, if they did not do any or all of the above, they are not LOOKING for me. Besides, you can only look for something that is "lost." The majority of the work day, I am where I am supposed to be, with whom I am supposed to be, and doing what I am supposed to be doing. As you can tell, I do not have any patience for coworkers who are haters that attempt to take any opportunity to blemish a high performer's reputation due to their own laziness, lack of effort, or incompetency.

So unless you are a slacker (*you can lie to me, but not to yourself*) do not let others at work imply joking wise or otherwise that they were looking for you. As far as my location and the location of most hardworking employees during work hours, others only need to attempt to SEEK and they shall FIND.

pass the whine (Cont'd)

pass the whine (Cont'd)

VINEYARD VIEW

Employees should use their words wisely when speaking about another employee. Most misunderstandings regarding an employee's whereabouts is due to lack of knowledge or effort. The focus of trying to protect your own reputation may unfortunately and unnecessarily damage the reputation of someone else. It is often helpful to protect yourself from these situations by communicating your whereabouts to a couple of individuals that will be your alibi if needed.

Grapes of Wisdom

A. Be clever enough to make good assumptions, but wise enough to think beyond what you can see.

B. People will assume the task to create a perception of you, but it's your job to manage it.

Caution: Please Do Not Touch

The words, "Please, Do Not touch" are usually displayed on fragile, valuable, and breakable items. However, there are also some employees within the workplace who have this sign hanging over their heads. The sign is invisible and the meaning is different. These individuals are secretly known in the workplace as the "untouchables." Everyone has met one of the untouchables even if their identity was unknown. The three main characteristics of an untouchable employee are the following:

1) The "untouchable" card is played during a situation when they know they are wrong, but double dare you to do anything about it.

2) It is obvious to everyone that these type of people are incompetent at their job, but for some reason they have been in the position for a while.

3) Most employees have had a run-in with this person only to find themselves severely punished or fired (cleverly sending a sign or warning to the rest of the work population that they should not mess with this individual).

When I was new to the working world, I was one of the unfortunate individuals who was unaware of this specific category of employees. It took a few negative and painful battles to come to the conclusion that these type of employees will always win in the end. It seems as though they are calling the shots and getting support from a higher level. There have been many discoveries in my career that uncovered the mystery behind the "do what I want or else" mentality of the untouchables. Some discoveries include: the person has information that could put a leader or the company in jeopardy; the person is an incompetent relative of a leader; the person is in a nonprofessional and inappropriate relationship with a high authority (*And you know what type of relationship to which I am referring*); or it could also be a source outside of the company that is pulling the strings through this untouchable person and being a professional or personal threat to an internal leader. There are many reasons that an employee is labeled as untouchable, but they will without a doubt fit into one of these categories.

Whenever you are faced with a confrontation with one of these individuals, you should RUN...... fast and far (*That is, if you value your job or your career*). Running can mean bowing down, apologizing without cause, or taking cover to avoid this individual completely. I realize that this is unfair, but true corporate concern only kicks into high gear if something is illegal and risky. Therefore, we must fend for ourselves and heed the warnings of the untouchables because they are definitely strolling through our corporate halls singing "You Can't Touch This."

pass the whine

pass the whine (Cont'd)

VINEYARD VIEW

Nepotism, favoritism, and discrimination are all frowned upon negatively at most companies whenever employees are brave enough to communicate this type of treatment with proof. However, the magic word is proof. It is always important to have fact-based examples when you are complaining about these subjective areas in your workplace. Multiple examples involving different individuals will also prove to be more convincing since one-off situations with one or two individuals may simply be viewed as a misunderstanding or a mere coincidence.

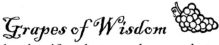

Grapes of Wisdom

Be careful to honestly classify what *you know*, what *you may not know*, and what *you think you know*- then proceed with caution.

The Craziness of it All

Day in and day out, we find ourselves trying to figure out this rat race roller coaster that we define as our workplace. Many people are working under both stress and fear due to the current economic times. Companies have demonstrated that they can hire new employees that will do more work for less pay. It seems as though companies are holding an invisible and unspoken threat in front of the best and brightest employees to encourage them to continue to do extra work out the fear of being the next chosen one to exit the company.

I personally and professionally feel that living or working in fear is not an option. I realize that superiors, leaders, and co-workers have their moments when they push you to the limit. They may even seem crazy at times. Instead of working in fear, your energy should be put into becoming "the employee with the answers", "the only one that knows how to….", or "the only employee willing to do this or that task". This strategy will decrease your fear that the company will ask you to leave while increasing the company's fear that you may choose to leave instead.

Once you position yourself in one of the previously stated situations and employers are on your last nerve, you can make them aware that you DO have the option to work elsewhere. If you are a stellar employee, they will not allow you to be worried away and create the chances of not having anyone else to take over your unique responsibilities. Besides, they may be crazy, but they are not stupid….and trust me, there is a difference.

pass the whine

pass the whine (Cont'd)

pass the whine (Cont'd)

pass the whine (Cont'd)

VINEYARD VIEW

Although employees may not always feel appreciated at an organization, companies are often aware of high performing employees who are valuable assets to the business. Since these employees are typically hardworking, type-A individuals that rarely say NO, it is often easy for co-workers and supervisors to take advantage of their work/life balance. Therefore, these individuals do not realize that they have the knowledge and performance to leverage reasonable push back at work.

Instead of taking precautions not to burn out, these employees choose to be pleasers which allows them to retain their title of supermen or superwomen. If you do not manage your own work/life balance, it will definitely not be balanced to your advantage by others. Companies and co-workers will continue to do what is best for them. So, you will have to take the wheel to do what is best for you.

Making a decision, in your favor, that will not have a negative impact on the business will never be a reason for a company to jeopardize a high performer's employment. Remember, push-back is different from insubordination. Push-back is deciding an alternative way to achieve similar results while insubordination is being totally defiant while unconsciously pursuing unemployment.

Grapes of Wisdom

Valuing the people that work hard for you is like giving the "hand that feeds you" a manicure.

When They Fake It, You Don't Make It

In today's job market, many people are interviewing for the first time in the last 8-15 years or the last 20 years for some. Regardless of how long ago it's been since your last interview, I'm sure you experienced the same anxiety as you did when you were far less experienced than you are now. I have met many types of interview candidates. They range from the shy and timid to the cocky and know it all. Fortunately, the current interviewing population has fallen comfortably in the middle. These middle type candidates are qualified, they know how to dress, and they know how to answer and ask appropriate questions.

Although great talent is out there, companies are still finding it difficult to identify the right candidate choice which leaves unemployed candidates puzzled about the many rejections they are getting from interviews. I know how these talented, rejected candidates feel because I have been there. Once you get your rejection message, you replay the interview over and over in your head trying to determine when it went bad. Allow me to spare you some agony by reassuring you that it is not always a mistake on your part. You may have done everything right. Just know that everyone that is interviewing you does not necessarily have the expertise to interview correctly.

When a hiring manager has an opening, he/she is the person with the highest stakes in the candidate selection. Therefore, the rest of the interviewing team is appointed or given a subpoena to assist with interviewing someone else's candidate (when *their team probably needs additional help as well, but the head count was not approved).* The commitment of being an interviewer will knowingly take 2-3 hours or sometimes days out of your schedule, depending on the role and the number of candidates. Unfortunately, this may put the interviewing candidates in situations where they are feeling the negative impact of this unwanted task at no fault of their own.

You may get interviewed by the person who will be harder on you because that person is not good at anything else, so they want to be the hard rock when it comes to interviewing. You may get the person who has never interviewed anyone before, but was unable to get out of doing it this time as they have been able to do in the past. Unfortunately, the feedback from this type of interviewer will also be accepted, although they were practicing inept interviewing skills on you.

Lastly, you may have the privilege to interview with someone who is very important and busy, which means that this interviewer was probably too busy to give you a thorough interview. As a result, this busy type of interviewer will rush the process and blame missing data on your inability to sell yourself.

If you are fortunate enough to avoid the three aforementioned types of interviewers, you will have a great interview experience with a qualified interviewer that will cause you to leave the interview feeling valued, heard, and knowledgeable of the role, even if you do not get the position.

It is bad enough that candidates have to update their resume, put on a suit, research the company, take time to go to the interview-only to discover that their preparation was in vain because they are being interviewed and evaluated by a counterfeit interviewer. So I say to these bad interviewers….People out there need a job!... So don't fake it until you make it because we can no longer take it.

pass the whine

pass the whine (Cont'd)

pass the whine (Cont'd)

VINEYARD VIEW

Interviewing is an art. A great interview requires skill from the interviewer to ask the right questions and skills from the interviewee or candidate to portray their experience relative to the desired role. It is important for both interviewer and candidate to be prepared in advance.

Candidates should gage the interview to determine if the interviewer is gaining appropriate information to make a good evaluation. It is appropriate for candidates to provide information in addition to answers of asked questions. The goal of the candidate is to ensure that he/she provides the interviewer with information that demonstrates that he/she meets all of the requirements, has experience or cross-over skills to perform all of the job duties, and has additional advantages over other candidates that may be interviewing for the same position. Unfortunately, your first impression on an interview is your last impression. So, over-prepare and be able to steer the interview in a direction that will benefit your desired goal during the interview whether you are the candidate or the interviewer.

Grapes of Wisdom

Sometimes the people who "know" are at the mercy of the people who "do not know".

Breakfast Is Served

Have you ever had to work with someone that thought he knew everything? I don't mean only everything about their individual work responsibilities, but *everything:* everything that they are working on, everything that you are working on, everything that is happening in the company, everything that is going on outside of the company, how things were before they were at the company, how things work now, and how things will be after they leave the company. I mean they think they know **E-V-E-R-Y-T-H-I-N-G!**

Don't get me wrong, I am very impressed and respectful of knowledgeable employees that are constantly bringing value to the organization. However, I also feel that there is always an opportunity for the same people to obtain information from others who may have additional facts or experience in a particular area. It is usually the individuals with the lowest self-esteem that try to shield themselves with the "All-knowing" uniform of armor. But, there are surely topics these "know-it-alls" prove to definitely indeed know "nothing about nothing".

The best way to coach the "know it all" type of employee is through live demonstrations. The next time this person is being absolutely sure about something that is incorrect, you should give him one friendly opportunity to be corrected by you. Once they have denied your knowledge (*which they always do)* and stand their ground, let it go. Let it go until the conversation has come to the defining point of action and until he has a captive audience.

Then you should politely, professionally, and joyfully explain that you tried to inform them at an earlier date that the facts regarding the issue are blah, blah, blah. Then you send them a mental message asking if they would like to have a side of bacon to go with the egg that's all over their face when they have to retract previous statements. Awwwhhh…… A breakfast made for THEM that will fuel YOU for the rest of the day.

pass the whine

pass the whine (Cont'd)

pass the whine (Cont'd)

VINEYARD VIEW

Having knowledge is a valuable employee asset in any organization. However, it is easy to get overly possessive when you are in charge of an important assignment, a big project, or a presentation at work. Although information that is volunteered is sometimes questionable, it is always wise to evaluate suggestions and advice from co-workers. Sometimes unsolicited advice may come across as snooping, stepping on your toes, or even sabotage. However, you can always decide not to use the advice, but listening prior to making a judgment call is vital. Successful people will always need help from others. When you portray yourself as a "know it all" and fail to see the value in each employee, people will not only refrain from sharing their creative opinions; moreover, they will also refrain from sharing critical facts that may protect you from your next fall.

Grapes of Wisdom

Since everyone knows something about certain things and no one knows everything about all things, there are endless opportunities to teach and to learn.

Diamond in the Rough

If you have ever had the opportunity to train or manage someone that is not exactly the whole talent package for a specific role, you will be able to relate to this message. I am a softy when it comes to proving to the world that every employee has value to be developed into just about any level. I have spent hours, days, weeks, months, and years coaching individuals to uncover their professional side. I see many talented employees who are savvy with the technical package only to discover that their style of communication, management, or attire is unsatisfactory. I agree that it is important for employees to have qualifications behind the scene but the professional side of an individual contributes to both the credibility and persuasion factor when in front of others. Therefore, I often feel that my coaching and advice to these employees provide a huge value to the company.

This is how I felt prior to having the following epiphany. After a year of coaching a particular individual, I had only refined his professional shine when I was present to hold him at a certain angle in the appropriate light without allowing anyone to examine him too closely. I realize that all the polishing in the world is not going to uncover a diamond when I was really working with a Cubic Zirconium! When real diamonds are discovered, they will make you proud in and out of your presence.

Diamonds are reliable and shine forever; costume jewelry will eventually tarnish hindering the reputation of both the trainee and the mentor. So before you begin your next assignment of bringing someone to the next level, you should identify what you are working with and acknowledge that individual's true potential.

pass the whine

pass the whine (Cont'd)

pass the whine (Cont'd)

VINEYARD VIEW

The workplace is a great environment to become either a mentor or a mentee. Mentoring will take on a different meaning depending on the participating employees. Some leaders are required to mentor an employee who is in a lower position. Therefore, be aware of leaders that come to you as an unsolicited mentor unless your organization has a structured development/ career path program. These programs have a process that assigns leaders as mentors to identified High Potential (Hi-Po) employees with similar gender, race, or career tracks. If this type of initiative does not exist at your organization, your volunteer mentor may only be checking a box on his own performance review by obtaining a mentee.

Unfortunately, when the mentor has not bought into the true benefits of being a mentor, these forced, non-motivated relationships will typically result in non-committed mentors and frustrated mentees. It is totally acceptable and suggested for an employee to identify a leader as a mentor. Ensure that this leader has demonstrated the professional success that you aspire to accomplish in the future. In addition, also ensure that you have proven yourself as a worthy mentee. Once the relationship is accepted and agreed upon, there should always be an initial discussion about the motives, objectives, and expectations of the mentoring relationship to prevent wasted time or a jaded reputation for either the mentor or the mentee.

Grapes of Wisdom

Change is the result of showing temporary differences in front of others. Transformation is the result of making permanent differences when no one is around. Why change?-TRANSFORM.

Corporate Allergies

I realize that there are certain duties and people at work that cause us to have a negative physical reaction. The level of dislike is usually in direct correlation with our body's reaction. Some of these reactions are mostly blamed on other things such as colds, bad meals, sinus issues, headaches, hunger, etc. Some people will also associate the reactions to allergies because of the symptoms of shortness of breath, hives, or digestion issues. It is hard to explain the feeling that occurs when you know you have to face an undesirable task or when you need to deal with an unbearable person. It usually begins with a sigh or massive blowing.

Next, you typically begin to voice your displeasures regarding the issue under your breath. You then attempt to do a mental search on how you can avoid the situation (*maybe pass it on to someone else or put it off until a later date*). And then ...before you know it, some part of your body (*that was perfectly fine prior to the negative news of the task*) begins to illustrate your displeasure as a negative body reaction of some sort.

A great example is when I get a pit in my stomach every time I discover an employee has lied, mistreated a direct report, or left a trail of discouraging evidence for a lawsuit that could put the company under the jail. I know this will create a painstaking employee relations issue that I will need to resolve.

An additional comparison is the emotion that I feel once I'm aware that I have digested one of the many foods that causes me to have an allergic reaction. So if I use an allergy analogy, a corporate allergy should be considered as a severe allergy, especially since this particular allergy cannot be controlled with Zyrtec, Benadryl, or an Epi-pen.

If you know that you also have a corporate allergy, you should acknowledge it and attempt to avoid it through environmental control. Being in HR, I think it is only fair that you include your corporate allergies during an interviewing process. Most resumes should read bold and clearly at the top (**Caution: Severely Allergic to Corporate Nuts**).

pass the whine

pass the whine (Cont'd)

pass the whine (Cont'd)

VINEYARD VIEW

In the workplace, there are many times that you will be required to work with people whom you find to be difficult or required to do assignments that you dislike. Unfortunately, you most likely will not have control over your co-workers or your assignments. However, you can control managing your reaction or attitude of any unpleasant work experiences.

Many legitimate illnesses that begin at work are due to stress. In order to prevent undue stress, it is important to provide the necessary feedback, responses, or adjustments to remove you from the victim's seat. As long as you feel as though someone or something is happening to you in a negative way, you will feel trapped, out of control and, therefore, stressed. This reaction will lead to anything from a headache, cold or to something as severe as an ulcer or disease (most diseases emanate in the body from stress or a lack of ease). When you take action to better the circumstance, your body will react in a more positive manner.

Grapes of Wisdom

Initially, situations will either affect your mind, body, or spirit. But, since all three are connected, each will be affected eventually.

Slick Willies

Day in and day out, all through the week, one year to the next__ time goes on as employees secretly and cleverly get away with acts that range from not doing work, to breaking policy/rules, to cheating on expense reports, etc. It is difficult for leaders and HR to monitor every act within the company at all times. Some corporations attempt to control many wrongful actions through random audits, security cameras, inventory control, and the like. In many instances, most negative acts are discovered accidentally due to sloppy execution on the employee's part.

Being in HR, I am rarely surprised by the insane actions of employees who (*for some reason*) do not think they are being watched by others. Let's be real for a moment. What is going through the minds of employees (*or your mind, if I am calling you out*) who go school supply shopping at work (*companies know this occurs July-Sept. every year, so they budget for it*) or those who run their Internet business from their office computer *(larger companies with IT departments usually run reports on sites visited and the amount of time at each site)*? This list of actions can go on and on, but my point is that companies are watching and are aware (*well at least, they are now if they are reading this book*).

Companies analyze data to determine if the effort of pursuing these short-lived, one-off acts are worth the dollar amount or manpower that it would take to have their eyes on everything at all times. Most successful companies prefer to keep their eyes on the prize and not be thrown off course by these small annoyances. In the past, many companies decided that they had bigger fish to fry.

However recently, the economy has forced companies to cut costs by all means and to have a tighter grip on their purse strings. Therefore, employees should think twice before going to the work supply cabinet to provide their households with toilet paper, school/office supplies, coffee, Lysol, or trash bags. Employees should also be careful about doing certain things at work such as international personal calls, personal Internet use to shop or pay bills, business postage for mailing, church bulletin/program copies, or purchasing personal items/ trips on corporate credit cards. Trust me when I say this list was not made up. I have developed it over the years through experience.

So if I have described you or a friend at work (*since no one wants to admit to being a corporate free loader*), take this as a warning prior to being professionally informed, embarrassingly approached, and straight out busted at work because" Willie, you are NOT slick."

pass the whine

pass the whine (Cont'd)

pass the whine (Cont'd)

pass the whine (Cont'd)

VINEYARD VIEW

Stealing is hardly the description used when time or items are taken from the workplace. Many people view it as an obligation of the company to provide these extra unspoken or unwritten fringe benefits.

Most companies are not concerned with a brief personal phone call, a box of tissues for the sudden sniffles for your long commute, or an envelope for the safekeeping of your necklace that was broken at work.

Corporations usually frown upon those people who are way out of control and decide to shop through their organization as if it is Office Depot, Staples, or Best Buy. A bottle of Lysol here, a ream of copy paper there, or just a mere box of staples or ballpoint pens may be the beginning of a more lucrative stash. The odds of you being approached regarding office theft increases with each act so just be aware that the company may or may not say anything, but someone is always looking.

Grapes of Wisdom

Every action has a consequence. The consequence may be big, small, sooner, later, direct, or indirect, but it will always exist.

Robbed by the Job

For those of you who have an ounce of Christian religion, I know you have heard the Biblical question, "Will a man rob God?" (If not, you are overdue for a Sunday school lesson). My question to you is "will a job rob you?"

When I was naïve and less experienced, I was certain that authority figures and large respected entities were above the low level act of robbery. Don't get me wrong; I was aware of the high dollar crimes such as embezzlement and money laundering, etc. However, I see within the workplace the act of "robbing" in a lower category of slowly "Nickel and Diming" vs. the fast one-time high dollar "stick 'em up" situations.

Having access to compensation data, time approval information, travel expense data, and the like, I observed how many employees at a lower pay structure, work their 8 hours, take all their breaks and lunches while ensuring that they do not come into work a minute early nor leave a minute late. I used to have a problem with this mentality because I viewed it as unmotivated, not career-oriented, or lacking ambition regarding the corporate ladder.

Now that I have made it to a higher salaried level, I see things differently. Most people who are in the higher salary bands work about 50-60 hours a week or more if they would be honest enough to count all the travel time, PDA checks, work conversations outside of work hours, work questions during vacation days, and the frequent weekend work. If a non-exempt (hourly worker) clocked in the same number of hours as a salaried employee and calculated the appropriate time & a half overtime or double-time overtime rate (for holidays), these hourly paid individuals would clearly make a salary that is probably close to, if not more than some salaried employees.

If you are an overworked salaried employee, you should take a deep breath and be brave enough to calculate your true hourly rate. You may decide to take a lower paying job that would allow you to have a life outside of work. I know some of you are saying ,"I love my job, and I don't have a problem with it being my entire life" or "The economy is bad and besides, hard workers don't get laid off". Well unless you work for your own business, the responses above can be accurately described as DENIAL. If you believe hard work and long hours are your safety net from unemployment, you will also most likely be the same person on the news ready to jump off a building if you get laid-off.

So, I know the truth hurts and it's less stressful to assume that you are getting paid appropriately for your time, your knowledge, and the value that you add to the company. However, think of it this way, if you do not look out for yourself, no one else will look out for you when it comes to your working hours out-weighing your pay.

Therefore, you should know how much time you are putting into work and know what your time is worth. Besides, if a man will rob God, any one of us can be a victim of corporate robbery.

pass the whine

VINEYARD VIEW

The best time to know what you are worth is during salary-offer negotiations. It is difficult for employees to catch up to an appropriate salary once they are in the organization. In addition, it is sometimes difficult to predict the amount of time that you will work in and out of the office.

The best advice is to do your research on your position prior to accepting a new salary to ensure that you will be appropriately paid for your time. If you are already an employee with a fixed salary, it is up to you to adjust and manage your work hours since this is the only variable in your control as a salaried employee. Knowing your value while having chosen work hours will allow you to set deadlines and expectations that will prevent you from feeling burnt out or taken advantage of by your corporation. This will create a pleasant work experience for you and a long term employee for the corporation.

Grapes of Wisdom

You should monitor how others utilize your time as you would if they were utilizing your money.

Corporate Kryptonite

For the most part, corporations are the "Super Entities" that they represent themselves to be.

They usually have the man-power, intellectual power, and financial power to make leaps in a single bound. Many employees feel powerless when faced with the decision to fight back after being wronged by bad bosses within a corporate giant.

Although assisting employees is my passion, I am also glad to assist a company in protecting itself from corrupt employees (A.K.A Corporate Hustlers) who are out to sue companies for no cause or to tarnish long standing corporate reputations just to gain the following: extra time off work (*usually time enough to allow HR to complete their termination papers*); a severance package (*funds that will usually run out before you are able to find the next job*); or a low dollar settlement pay-out (*usually negotiated by a sleazy lawyer who is not competent enough to take cases that will require real legal talent or effort*).

Throughout the years, I have gained gratification helping the upstanding employees who have been given a raw deal. For example, these employees include those who are being targeted for no reason beyond petty personality differences or corporate politics. Or even more interesting, those employees who have been sexually harassed or discriminated against, but are trying to lay low to keep their job.

It is sad that the employees that want to do the right thing are rarely educated on how to battle a bad boss. On the other hand, the corporate hustlers are more in tune with the boundaries of the corporation (*they must have HR law books as bedside reading*). It is time that the high performing, upstanding employees protect themselves with HR education. The following accusations, if documented and communicated, will stop a bad boss in his/her tracks and get the monkey off your back. These issues include harassment, discrimination (sexual orientation, gender, age or race), retaliation, or any non-compliant issue (state, industry, or government related).

All of these forms of discrimination are able to paralyze a boss from attacking you with any further "Superman-get out of my way-I can do whatever I like" actions. So if you are going against a super boss and you are ready to FIGHT, you better bring...... the KRYPTONITE!!!!.

pass the whine

pass the whine (Cont'd)

pass the whine (Cont'd)

VINEYARD VIEW

Corporations as a whole are often wise enough to abide by civil and employee laws for their own protection. Most HR employees will welcome information that will allow them to address issues dead-on that could possibly prevent a legal suit from occurring. All of the state, government labor, and employee laws are enforced to protect every employee regardless of race, age, gender, or sexual orientation. It is wise to speak up when you feel as though you are being mistreated at work in any way.

However, you should be very careful not to make any false accusations. Companies will subconsciously react to pranksters by preventing them from sticking around too much longer after feathers have been ruffled with frequent unjustifiable accusations. Communicate the facts of the situation and allow HR to come to the obvious conclusions. Companies will usually address the issue to prevent you from making any future aligations.

If you have a legitimate complaint, please remember that you are also protected by law from retaliation for voicing the complaint. So, if you are going to put in a legitimate complaint, you should not be afraid if you stick to the facts and have your concerns and complaint well documented for future discussions with HR, corporate counsel, external lawyers, EEOC, or any other party that would be interested in hearing the facts of the case.

Grapes of Wisdom

Silent cries for help will produce invisible assistance.

The volume of your concern determines your priority number on someone else's to-do list.

Business 101— For Smarty Pants

As we travel along our career journey, we begin to listen to what we want to hear, look at what we want to see, and believe in corporate fairy dust and unicorns.

In other words, we seem to have forgotten business basics.

It is amazing how much time and money we spend on education, business courses, MBAs, and certificates to still get burnt with business deals, job offers, and customer contracts. If followed continuously under "any and every" circumstance, there is a rule that will prevent the above torching. Most mishaps regarding contracts, promises, or agreements occur when this small, but very important rule is ignored or forgotten.

"If you get it in writing, it is true. If you fail to do so, then it's all on you." (*Remember: In God we trust, all others need a signed agreement*).

pass the whine

pass the whine (Cont'd)

VINEYARD VIEW

Written agreements are necessary to benefit all involved parties. The workplace is constantly changing due to re-organizations, terminations, business needs, budgets, and other unforeseen circumstances. Therefore, what is willingly promised one day may be seen as unreasonable, inconvenient, or unnecessary at a future date. Some people feel uncomfortable requesting agreements or promises in writing. This act can be seen as an act of mistrust if presented in the wrong way. You should always frame up these types of requests to be beneficial to all parties. Therefore, written agreements should be written to hold all parties to certain commitments to represent a win-win situation. It's really that simple- Class Over.

Grapes of Wisdom

Verbal agreements are like writing on an "Etch 'n Sketch". The agreement exist until things are shaken up a bit.

Look Like a Butterfly, Sting Like a Bee

It usually occurs out of the blue. It typically catches you off guard. You could be on a phone call, in the middle of a meeting, or sitting at your desk minding your business.

And then.............. BAM!!!!!! Someone at work decides to "try you". Now most of the time this sudden act happens because something has occurred or is about to occur that will make them look, feel, or sound dumb. They usually come to you talking some kind of crackernacker bull as if you are crazy enough to sit there and take it lying down. These co-workers are usually testing your willpower, professionalism, and in some cases, your religion.

Most people would think it is easy enough to handle these trying situations by speaking as adults and informing one another of our personal expectations of professional communication. Well, in most cases, this is true. However, there are other cases that require you to provide a response that will be shocking, eye-opening, jaw dropping, and memorable enough to teach an instantaneous life-lesson of how not to "try" you without thinking twice.

I realize that we are all adults. Therefore, the childish street response of "Yo Mama" is probably not the best choice (*even if appropriate*). I have found that most people have not mastered the skill of profoundly, but professionally "checking" a coworker. People who try you are most likely to be inexperienced cowards who are calling your bluff by saying

142

or doing something that will cause you to over react, turn the tables, and paint themselves as the victim who crossed your evil path.

Although the saying, "Don't start none, won't be none" is true, please do not take this bait. The most important part of a corporate "let me set you straight" conversation is to get your point across in a professional and non-threatening way. If you fail at this task, you will know immediately since the student of your lesson will run to HR crying crocodile tears while claiming that you have threatened them badly and that you create a hostile work environment.

So if you choose your words, gestures, and location carefully, you can master these trying conversations with a TKO while avoiding all the pitfalls. Once this occurs, your contenders will walk away trying to determine if they were cursed out since your smile and word choice will confuse them. However, your successful round in the corporate boxing ring should have them thinking, "I better back down, before I get smacked down".

pass the whine

pass the whine (Cont'd)

VINEYARD VIEW

Corporations expect their employees to present themselves in a professional manner at all times. There is no exception if someone says or does something that is totally inappropriate or unnecessary. Although inappropriate statements are often made in the workplace, many people are wise enough to stay right above the line of unacceptable behavior while going below the line of irritation. As adults, you must learn to address these situations in a manner that will gain you respect and future cooperation from those who are not appropriately communicating with you.

Grapes of Wisdom

The tongue can be the most lethal muscle in the body when the mind and heart are disengaged.

"Just Do It Now"

"Slackers"! We all know at least one. They exist throughout the workplace. Where did they come from? How did they get hired? Why haven't they been fired? (Well, they are probably not being fired because they are the first to yell "FOUL" *(in the form of discrimination, harassment, or retaliation)* when their performance is challenged in any way. They are pros at delivering complaints and issues, but will never contribute solutions. They are often out sick *(usually conveniently on Monday or Friday to extend their weekend)*.

Slackers are not ashamed of their incompetent traits. They wear "Slackness" as a badge of honor to avoid assignments that require any effort. Many excuses are provided for why something will not work, why assignments are incomplete or late, or why it is just impossible or too difficult to get something done. So, I guess you are wondering, what's their secret? Well, I'm slowly figuring out this special breed of employees.

It's not due to one type of personality since slackers are chameleons that are able to transform into whatever is necessary to do less. Slackers can be so unbearable to be around that people will go out of the way not to include them in work assignments. Or, they can be so sociable that they hypnotize others into subconsciously covering for them and doing their work.

The slacker persona is puzzling because it typically demonstrates a clever and complex strategy to ensure that slackers are right above the line of getting fired and right below the line of being functional valuable

146

workers. I realize that slackers feel as though they are "getting over" by receiving a paycheck without doing work. But, why do they put all of this energy and effort into avoiding work when it would take less energy and effort to just do it!

pass the whine

pass the whine (Cont'd)

pass the whine (Cont'd)

VINEYARD VIEW:

It is not surprising that someone would attempt to avoid a painful assignment at work. However, the most successful working teams take the time to identify the strengths, weaknesses, desires, and annoyances of each member. Regardless of the task, there is a member on the team that would find it less painful, less challenging, or in some cases, even enjoyable. It is true that employees do their best work on a task that they find desirable.

Great team building exercises exist to identify information such as personality traits, work type preferences, strengths, weaknesses, and the like. Teams that take the time to evaluate their resources are far more productive than work teams that assign work assignments without guidance to ensure the team produces the best work. A team can reduce its slackers by ensuring work assignments are not avoided due to lack of competency or desire.

Grapes of Wisdom

Constantly re-doing bad work and avoiding hard work will only create a tired, over-worked, non-achiever.

A.S.A.P

A.S.A.P (aka as soon as possible). This term is often used in the workplace to identify tasks that need to be executed quickly. The original idea of the term probably started with good intentions. If used correctly, this term could be a polite way of saying, "Excuse *me fellow worker, I know that you are usually a diligent worker anyway. However, I know you have a lot on your plate, but I just wanted to make you aware of this particular task, since it should not fall through the cracks or sit on the back burner. Please do your best to complete it as soon as it is possible.*" Well somewhere down the line, many employees missed the memo of how to properly use the term. Therefore, A.S.A.P is so misused and overly used that its urgency has been watered down.

Typically when people receive an A.S.A.P message, it leaves a negative impact. Most people see it as a selfish way for the sender to say, "*Look man, I've sat on this for way too long and now the heat is on me to complete it. I know that I should have asked for this data a long time ago, —but if you stall on this, I'll have to throw you under the bus to cover my own sorry A_ _"*.

From another view point, a sender of the A.S.A.P term could be saying, "*Hey, I know how slow and lazy you are on delivering information, but you need to move on this task because it is very important to my job. I know you will come up with some lame excuse at the last minute of why you can't deliver, so I have actually shortened the due date to build in some cushion to keep both of us from getting fired, since I will surely take you with me.*"

Besides having multiple meanings, "As soon as Possible" can also have different timelines for different people. What is possible for you may not be possible for me. Since it is difficult to determine how the term will be perceived by different people, we should at least have clarifying responses to the term to ensure that the sender of A.S.A.P messages has a clue what to expect from us.

Some replies to the acronym A.S.A.P could be one of the following acronyms:

I.B.A.W- It'll be a while.
I.O.T.W- It's on the way.
T.N.M.P- Totally not my problem
T.Y.G.A- There You go again
Y.O.C.A- You're one crazy As_!

Regardless of your chosen response, it is important to know the true meaning of the acronym A.S.A.P. Although it initially meant "as soon as possible," it has transformed to mean "Act Suddenly- Address Problem" (not your problem, but my problem!!)

pass the whine

pass the whine (Cont'd)

pass the whine (Cont'd)

VINEYARD VIEW:

In today's society, time is a precious commodity. It's professional to respect the time of others and to insist that others respect your time as well. Some employees find themselves involved in situations that could have been avoided with appropriate communication.

Most co-workers or superiors will have a difficult time asking you to miss an announced personal responsibility unnecessarily or take the chance of having you destroy a task for them due to a loaded plate of projects that are publicly known without first justifying or explaining the importance and severity of their request. Additional communication will allow you to insert further logic into the conversation to determine if it is truly an urgent task or not. Therefore, you should require factual information and a specific time and date prior to accepting an ASAP task within the workplace.

Grapes of Wisdom

Whether they are arranged by you or by others, your priorities are always in a particular order at any given time.

Every Sense Counts

There are many corporate terms used to gain the thoughts, opinions, and professional advice of others. Some of these terms are collaboration, teamwork, brain storming, benchmarking, and the list goes on and on. An increased diversity of thought within a group will result in better ideas. The companies that are more innovative and creative have discovered how to make these data mining activities useful and successful.

Many leaders want to portray this inclusive mentality because it has a positive effect on the morale of their workforce when ideas are solicited and captured from every level. The leaders also want to be known as having a collaborative vs. authoritative management style. Regardless of the reason, ideas opinions, or advice within the workplace are sometimes solicited in vain. In some cases, leaders' words are saying one thing, but their actions are saying, "Whatever! This is what we're going to do regardless of what you think."

Because I'm in HR, many people do not ask me for advice to discover what they can or should do, but to discover what they can get away with doing without being penalized, sued, or fired. I'm all about providing guidance and information when it is requested by others. Unfortunately, some people will ask for your opinion when they are really looking for a partner in crime. They will go on a shopping spree until they finally receive an idea that coincides with what they were planning to do anyway.

When so many people are suffering from long work-hours and tight budgets, it seems as though the "check the box' mentality of "acting-like" you are including others would stop. If you really want to shorten your work day, stop wasting people's time by asking for information that you are going to ignore anyway. Do I stand to be corrected? Am I the only one who feels that advice is valuable? Let's practice common sense by valuing the sense of others.

The next time a co-worker or boss comes to solicit your thoughts in vain (*when they are going to do what they want to do anyway*), you can say, "Hello!, times are hard. I would rather save my 2 cents for a rainy day than to keep throwing them away."

pass the whine

pass the whine (Cont'd)

VINEYARD VIEW:

Everyone has valuable input at some point in time in their work environment. It is often easy for employees to judge their input based solely on how or if that input is utilized by the receiver. Unfortunately, we do not have control over what happens to our input once it is provided. Depending on the inquirer's maturity, knowledge, motive, or expectations, a responder's well intended input may be used, ignored, or labeled as invaluable. Therefore, it is important to emotionally detach yourself from solicited input by simply being content with knowing that you've done what was in your control.

Grapes of Wisdom

Wasted time, wasted money, or wasted advice is the result of a valuable resource that was managed in a negligent manner.

A Day Late and A Dollar Short

As employees double their workload, they begin to question if they are valued by their company. This value is typically displayed through public recognition, rewards, a salary increase, or a promotion (*of course there are verbal compliments as well, but must employees don't seem to hear these broken record comments since actions speak louder than words*).

Some companies now feel as though they have the upper hand due to the high unemployment rate and the sluggish economy. It is true that companies without a conscience are being foul while getting away with things that would not be tolerated by employees in a good economy.

Surprisingly, there are some exceptions of employees still having the upper hand at companies. For example, a friend of mine was called in to a meeting by her employer to discuss her role after a long period of being looked over for promotions and being ignored regarding pay raises. Anyway, they thought they were doing something special when they offered her a promotion. (*My guess is that a background employer history check probably tipped them off about her job search which led to this desperate, unexpected, out of the blue promotion*). However, she was able to respond to their promotion offer within the same day by turning in her resignation due to an external job offer. Bamm!! Umh! Take that! She left them with their mouths hanging wide open.

It's amazing how companies find you more desirable when another company is also interested in what you have to offer. (*Hence, this explains why it is easier to find a job when you already have one.*)

Regardless of the economy, you should continue to do your best at your current job even if the company appears to be unworthy. Besides, it's just a matter of time before you find a better opportunity -- that is "A Day Early and a Dollar longer".

pass the whine

pass the whine (Cont'd)

pass the whine (Cont'd)

VINEYARD VIEW:

Human nature causes all of us to get satisfaction when the underdog becomes victorious. However, the workplace makes it difficult to be victorious unless it is a win-win situation. A slacker or incompetent worker who gets a promotion is a loss to the company. On the contrary, a high performer who continues to be overlooked for a promotion is a loss for the employee and eventually the company as well. Open, fair, logical, and compassionate communication is the key to a win-win scenario between executives and staff.

Staff should realize that business is a corporation's top priority. Moreover, the corporation should realize that a happy hard working staff is the key to a successful business. Although many believe that a line is drawn between the leadership and the staff within most organizations, it is extremely difficult, if not impossible, for one of these groups to negatively affect the other without negatively impacting themselves and the company as a whole. The main objective should be to keep the company thriving while allowing both leadership and staff to benefit from the company's success.

Grapes of Wisdom

Win-win situations = C^3: Commitment, Creativity, and Collaboration by all involved parties.

Help Wanted-
"Hatetologist"-Manager

B ased on the whine collections thus far, you may have it twisted by mistaking the "shots of realism" as negativity. The truth of the matter is that there are positive people who are aware of negative things while striving to move forward in spite of them. However, if you choose to be a Pollyanna by avoiding the discussion of negative situations, you may be obliviously walking on the train tracks when the train is on the way. I personally choose to take the route of listening for the train while walking on the tracks of life so I can stay informed and know when to jump onto the platform.

Regardless of how you manage negativity, a negative culture is plaguing the current workplace. Many individuals are going through a host of negative emotions at work. The economy, heavy workloads, bad bosses – you name it, all of these issues have been blamed for undesired emotions at work. Because we spend the majority of our waking hours on a job, you would think that our workplace could provide some sort of peace, faith, or reassurance that things will turn for the better and that there are still good people in this world. Most people feel that the Human Resources department should take ownership of this positivity task and walk around work singing "Kumbaya My Lord, Kumbaya".

Although I think HR should be a beacon of light to the workplace, the hands of HR are tied due to law, policy, harassment, and discrimination which force most HR staff to remain stoic and to appear heartless. There have probably been numerous conversations where HR wanted to tell

166

the employee – "Dag, your situation is jacked up. If I were you, I would be crying too." HR has also had the urge to secretly inform employees that they were headed for trouble or that they were being set up for a fall, but employees are so thrilled to have an inside scoop that they would most likely blab their confidential HR conversations (*adding two additional headcount to the unemployment line*).

Unfortunately, the safest option of a HR professional is to suggest the company's confidential Employee Assistant Program (EAP) (*and by the way, it really is confidential-since some people truly believe that your employee folder is stamped with the word CRAZY if you ever utilize the assistance program for emotional stress.*)

The truth of the matter is that we can ALL help each other by decreasing intentional un-pleasantries within our workplace. Is it possible to stop the back biting, back stabbing, bus throwing, and blackballing completely? Let's face it, most workplace misery is in our control and is caused by our co-workers. We need to do whatever possible to shine a new light on how we play this corporate game.

I see the human values of this workforce sliding down a slippery sloop. I realize that misery loves company, but I'm asking if we can adjust our attitudes to bring someone up instead of holding someone down. So, if you are up for the role and qualified for the "Hatetologist"-Manager assignment, the job is yours! Go to work and give it a try while avoiding both the Haters and their Hater-aid.

pass the whine

pass the whine (Cont'd)

pass the whine (Cont'd)

VINEYARD VIEW:

The workplace is our home away from home, a place whose environment typically overflows with competition. Many misuse the urge to compete by incorporating a crab mentality. Some employees will decide that they can only be viewed as the more valuable employee if they make other employees look bad. These conniving employees make their fellow employees look bad by throwing them under the bus or by showcasing some of their co-worker's faults or weaknesses.

The other competition issue involves poor performers who have decided they are not willing to compete in the work performance arena, so they must identify additional ways to ensure that they have the spot light even if that spotlight is not deserved or earned in an ethical manner.

In today's workplace, you will only get but so far with experience and credentials if you do not have emotional intelligence, a keen sense of people skills, and extreme street smarts. The easiest way to differentiate yourself from the low performers is to discontinue the venting sessions, perform beyond the level of expectation, and associate with individuals who have already accomplished what you are striving to get.

You should also stay in the company of positive individuals since misery loves company. Surrounding yourself with the appropriate network will put you in the position of being mentored by individuals within your circle who do not see you as a threat. Although it is impossible to eliminate workplace Haters all together, you can surely aim to decrease the chances of intimidation or jealously within your working circle.

Grapes of Wisdom

If you do not have any Haters, you are surely doing something wrong; jealousy from others is one confirmation of achievement.

New Hire on the Block

It's a place that we have all visited at some time or another. It is the oblivious, vulnerable, uncertain place of being a new employee. You come into the new company or group excited about the new opportunity. You are ready to roll-up your sleeves to make a difference. You aim to justify both your value and your nice-new salary (*that you were hopefully brave enough to negotiate during the offer*). Everyone that you meet seems nice and helpful. All of your colleagues appear so knowledgeable (*especially since you are just learning the ropes*).

You are on a mission to make your boss proud and grateful that you were selected over all the other candidates. In the process of being an eager beaver, you overcommit, you say yes to everything, you get pulled into numerous projects, and you allow the noisy vultures to gain personal information that they will use against you later. This "new employee journey" is such a mirage that it totally disguises the chaos that you may have signed up for in your new role.

If you are coming into a newly created role, your biggest concerns will involve ensuring the proper structure of the role, knowing how it fits into the rest of the organization, and defining the scope of your responsibilities.

If you are replacing someone that was fired, your biggest challenge will be to clean up the mess that began the second this person mentally checked out of the role, which is usually long before they physically checked out.

If you are fortunate enough to replace a high performing employee who kept his/her "ducks in a row", your biggest challenge will be to fill this person's shoes while gaining buy-in for decisions that are different decisions than the ones of your prestigious predecessor.

My point is that all new employees will have to take this journey. Many employees recognize when they are in the honeymoon stage in the midst of this journey, but few remember how the journey ended. Allow me to enlighten you on when the journey ended.

Well, it probably was a single "moment-in-time" that resembled being in a dense fog. The once smiling faces began to look more like growls and snickering, and you began to resent all the people who put you on their projects. Your breathing became short and shallow because you finally realized that your workload was unrealistic. During meetings with your boss, you had a small vein that popped out on your neck because you now realize that your boss was clueless (*hence, the real reason that you were hired*).

In addition, you began monitoring every word when speaking with your colleagues and your CYA file was expanding far beyond its infancy stage. Then suddenly, out of nowhere, you saw a new face peeping through the fog. The new face said, "Hi, it is good to meet you. I'm new to the team."

Low and behold, your crown had been passed along to yet another person who will now explore the journey and assume the title of the "New hire on the block".

pass the whine

pass the whine (Cont'd)

VINEYARD VIEW:

The beginning of a work assignment is the most important stage of your journey at a new company or in a new group. The first impression will usually define your future reputation. It is important that you set the stage for the first 6-12 months to present your best work. Most new employees are so focused on doing tons of work that they lose focus of performing extremely well on the work assignments. If a new employee does great work on a few projects, it is assumed that he/she will do a great job on additional projects as well, once given the opportunity.

The lower number of projects will most likely be justified by your learning curve of the company, the team dynamics, or any new systems/processes. Therefore, you should not concentrate solely on the amount of work since this is the expectation for more tenured employees who are trying to demonstrate their long term value. In addition, a new employee should never shy away from asking follow-up questions by attempting to be viewed as a quick learner. The "New" title will be lost very quickly. Therefore, it should be utilized to your advantage and not used to allow others to take advantage of you.

Grapes of Wisdom

Your first observation of productivity as a new team member will most likely be your clearest perspective prior to having your view tainted with jaded explanations or excuses from existing team members.

Eye Candy

Is it true? I mean really true; do good looking people get the breaks at work? Well, I can give you an honest and well contemplated answer in two words….Of Course!!!

I'm not saying that is fair, right, or even legal, but I am saying that it's true. I have seen several articles on the topic of attractiveness in the workplace. Most of the articles are cleverly remaining politically correct by stating that the employer is concerned with the face of the employee since that face will be the face of the company in the eyes of the client. I say, Whatever!!!! There may be a small percentage of truth to this theory if we were only speaking about sales people. However, this theory falls short when you consider other positions within a company that do not have access to the external customer.

Being in HR, I have sat in numerous interview discussions where I could guess which candidates would not make it to the round two interviews based on how their looks stacked up against the other candidates. A possible explanation for this mindset is that people want to work with good looking people because they feel that this will increase their own looks in some magical way. However, it totally depends on the judging audience, since there are also haters who want to punish anyone that might have skated through life due to their good looks. In this case, the good looking people are always hassled and harassed with jokes regarding their perfections and abilities to handle failure.

Although I can think of many industries other than television and outside sales where physical appearance or "looks" could justifiably make or break an employee (*the industries that come to mind require bunny ears, a street corner, or perhaps a pole*), I do not understand how looks can trump knowledge in the corporate workplace.

I do not know about you, but I would prefer a competent person on my project team versus someone who is looking good and looking dumb. Of course, the best choice is a royal flush of beauty and brains. If the choice has to be between two incompetent individuals where one is attractive and the other is unattractive, I would say... pick the eye candy. Besides even the unqualified Helens of Troy and the Narcissuses of the world should at least contribute to the beauty of the environment since they are taking up space, using up air, and knowing "nothing about nothing".

pass the whine

pass the whine (Cont'd)

pass the whine (Cont'd)

pass the whine (Cont'd)

VINEYARD VIEW:

Unfortunately there are many factors that are used in determining the chosen candidate. The decision should always be made to increase the performance of the company and the quality of work within the department. However, personal bias can often play a part, even if it is subconsciously. Interviewers are either making a selection from the viewpoint of "I aspire to be as good as this candidate one day"or "I do not want to increase my competition by hiring this candidate who has something better than me."

Hiring for the wrong reasons can only recreate more of the issues that the company is attempting to solve by filling the vacancy. Now that you realize that looks do play a factor in an interview, be sure to present your appearance and your experience in a thoughtful way. The best way to win over an interview is to display how you will improve the workplace experience for the interviewer once you come on board. Also, if you are the interviewer, be conscious of the motives and long term consequences while selecting a new hire.

Grapes of Wisdom

A beautiful attractive hire that is not qualified to do the job is like a nicely wrapped box without a gift. Neither is appreciated for long.

Monkey See, Monkey Do

For every action at work, there is not only a reaction, but a duplicate action. Although the workplace is assumed to be filled with adults, child-like syndromes are in full effect, such as "she got one, why not me" or "His/hers is bigger than mine". This childish mentality has companies, HR, and the government all jumping through hoops to ensure that all actions are carried out equally to all employees.

I am the first to say that all employees should be treated fairly, but the act of treating all employees "equally" has all of us running a muck. It is unfortunate that leadership doesn't have the parental power to say" It will be this way for you because…. "I said so". Oh, now that I think about it, this probably would not be a great idea since some leadership has proven not to have the same loving intentions of a parent (*to love all the kids the same even if they are treated differently per situation*).

My frustration with co-workers wanting the same as other co-workers is that they want to pick and choose the duplicate actions. I wouldn't have a problem with them if they wanted the same headaches, same long work hours, same workload, same commute, same title, same evaluation, same accountability, etc. But Noooooooooo, most of the complainers/haters only desire to have the same salary, same bonus, same work from home days, same flexible hours, same promotions, same office/equipment advantages (*even if their job or work ethic does not warrant it*).

Work is a hard enough jungle when we are worrying about the Guerilla (*Gorilla*) warfare and bullying apes, but now we have to also worry about the whining monkeys. Pleeeeease, give me a break!..but, by all means, be sure to give Susie a break too.

pass the whine

pass the whine (Cont'd)

pass the whine (Cont'd)

VINEYARD VIEW:

It is true that all employees should be treated with professionalism, respect, compassion, and rewards where applicable. However, all employees do not have the same needs at the same time. The best practice is to handle each situation with an equal level of care and concern. Companies should have practices or policies that are utilized in similar situations.

There should also be enough flexibility to allow companies to properly manage one-off situations without breaking labor laws or being accused of favoritism or discrimination. Although there are cases of favoritism within the workplace, it is rarely displayed in a blatant manner for all to see. Employees should evaluate an entire situation when they discover that certain rewards or incentives are being offered to other co-workers, but not being offered to them.

Grapes of Wisdom

Although some eat fish and others eat worms, some spend the day in the air, and some spend the day on a farm; all birds are birds. However, it is not considered fair, reasonable, or sensible to treat every bird nor everyone exactly the same while ignoring current needs and individual situations."

Fly On the Wall

Do you ever wonder what your boss is saying about you behind closed doors or at the decision table? Well, if you are not wondering, you should be. It amazes me how employees are led to believe that they have a good relationship with their boss, but the conversations had about them in their absence does not support their theory. Many decisions that affect you as an employee are communicated to your boss prior to making the decision final.

Many spineless bosses will try to act as though the undesired choices were out of their control. However, most bosses are given an opportunity to offer another decision or to prove why the suggested decision is not in the best interest of the business or the employee. Unfortunately, the success of these employee-related conversations rely solely on the backbone of your boss. The only way to ensure that bosses are looking out for your best interest is that the decision is also in their best interest.

You may be blessed with a boss that is wired to always do the right thing. Well in some cases, the decision may be right for the employee, but the wrong decision for the company or vice- versa. This would be an easy call for a spineless boss, but a tough call for a caring boss with a backbone. The truth is….. You will never really know the truth. Unless that is… you are a fly on the wall.

pass the whine

pass the whine (Cont'd)

VINEYARD VIEW:

It is very important that corporations allow each employee to determine what will benefit or adversely affect his/her personal life. The wise and less risky way to manage a possible work/life balance issue of an employee is to leave personal decisions and judgments up to the employee. Many employees, by disclosing all of their personal business, allow a corporation to make decisions that seem to be in their best interest.

Other employees are more private and leave the organization to guess or assume information about their lifestyles or personal matters.

Fortunately, if organizations are making decisions based primarily on an employee's performance, experience, or skill potential, it will not have the burden of making a decision based on any personal circumstances that may be correctly or incorrectly assumed.

Grapes of Wisdom

To either guess, assume, or think that you know someone's personal business may all lead you great distances from the truth.

Commuter's Combat Zone

Day in and day out, millions of people go to and from work using a variety of methods. If you are in a metro area, your choices expand beyond commuting by automobile. For Example, metro commuters have the choice of automobile, train, taxi, bus, bike, ferry, walking, or even helicopter (*if you happen to have it like that-because of your position or your bank roll*). It would seem that the more commuting options available, the easier the commute..... WRONG!!!! Regardless of how you get to work, if you have over a 30 minute commute, commuting is probably a constant pain. Due to the economy and the lack of jobs, many people have taken jobs that require them to WORK at getting to work.

Although I have personally had commuting nightmares, I also know others who have decided to take a much lengthier commute to have a particular job or to have a job at all for that matter. I have had the experience of working from my home, commuting 5-8 minutes, working out of a car all day, and memorable experiences of insanely lengthy commutes over an hour by car and train. All of these experiences have made me sensitive to commuting issues such as bad traffic, broken or cancelled trains and buses, as well as escalating fares, rude drivers/passengers/pedestrians. You name it, and someone at your workplace has had to go through difficulties and inconveniences to get to work.

Lengthy commutes are weighing heavily on our mental, emotional, physical, and financial health. Unfortunately, if you experience multiple commuting mishaps in a brief time period, this will most likely have a negative impact on the initial part of your day due to ranting and raving. I normally gripe about things in which I have a suggested solution. However, this issue has me at a loss. We need to get to work. Since every lengthy commute has its issues and we don't all have the luxury of working from home, I guess it.... just is, what it is.

pass the whine

pass the whine (Cont'd)

pass the whine (Cont'd)

pass the whine (Cont'd)

VINEYARD VIEW:

Many companies have attempted to ease some of the burden of commuters by implementing work days from home, flexible work hours, and commuting fee assistance or tax breaks. Some organizations are assisting commuters by organizing their facilities to increase the conveniences of every day needs to reduce the stress of a commuter's schedule. These conveniences may include drop off/pick-up cleaner service, exercise facilities, on-site daycare facility, free coffee/tea, laptops, PDAs, and so on. Most companies realize that any stress, anger or inconvenience that is caused by unfavorable commutes will be reflected in an employee's performance.

Unfortunately, these concerns are rarely considered by either the company or the employee during the hiring process or personal changes while on a job. In the midst of getting what we want, we want to believe that the commute is not that bad and that we will get used to it after a certain amount of time. This is true for some people, but not necessarily true for all people. Some of us are just initially doing what we believed we could do for the long term.

Grapes of Wisdom

Every now and then, sacrifices should be re-evaluated to prevent you from crossing the line of crazy.

Meeting-holics

I know that many companies have the issue of "meeting madness." People will have a meeting to prepare for a meeting that is a prerequisite for yet another meeting. I feel bad for the ones who have to stomach going to all of these meetings, but I feel worst for the people who have the responsibility of juggling different calendars to schedule all these meetings. Some people's calendars are actually booked with meetings all day long. So here's my question: when do they have time to do all of the work that is requested or assigned in the meetings?

In addition to having too many meetings, most meetings last way too long. I realize that the person that is requesting the meeting will usually *for the most part* have a plan for the meeting with a clear agenda. However, by the time everyone contributes their two cents *(or one cent for those who talk just to be talking)*, the meeting is thrown off schedule or the main topics are not discussed prior to the meeting's end, which requires a follow- up meeting. There should be a law against setting up recurring meetings on our work calendars. Seriously though, if you have something important enough to meet about, it should be important enough to schedule during the time it is needed and have the clout to bump any other event that may conflict.

Many companies are beginning to invest in expensive advanced communication systems to support the meeting overload through virtual meetings although most employees prefer to meet face to face. Also, conference calls have gained major popularity. However, the truth regarding these type of meetings for some people is that they have already categorized the conference call as "Crackernacker- bull" and are, therefore, not fully engaged (*or more professionally stated... they are multi-tasking*).

I'm not saying that meetings are not an important part of doing business. What I am saying is that meetings should be better scheduled, well planned, successfully facilitated, and only include the necessary participants.

So when your day is shot to hell, and there's no time to be truly productive, or you feel drained of energy without any results to show for your efforts, don't blame your boss, your co-workers, your time-management skills, or your workload. You can most likely blame it on the meetings!!!!!

pass the whine

pass the whine (Cont'd)

pass the whine (Cont'd)

VINEYARD VIEW:

Many hours and productivity are wasted on a daily basis within the workplace due to over scheduled and mismanaged meetings. Some employees have become so addicted to meetings that no decisions or steps are taken with a project prior to having a meeting. To avoid unnecessary meetings, employees should determine if an e-mail response from team members will be just as effective as pulling everyone from their additional work obligations.

Corporations implemented the concept of meetings to encourage collaboration, team work, diversity of thought, and innovation. However, it is possible for the same meetings that are scheduled to grow the company's business to also create a drain on the company's productivity and energy when they are misused. Once a meeting is necessary, be sure to have it properly scheduled with an agenda, the appropriate attendees, and for a specific time frame.

Grapes of Wisdom

Two heads are better than one, but too many opinions from others may paralyze your progress and create a multi-headed monster.

And the Oscar Goes to...

Deceit is rampant within the workplace. Most people should be given the benefit of the doubt by assuming they will only lie to protect themselves or someone else from the ridicule or judgment that could cause a tainted reputation or possible job elimination. Ok soooo, if anyone can volunteer false information to save a reputation or job, they can also volunteer false information that could cause tainted reputations or job eliminations for co-workers. However, lies also occur frequently on a casual basis when co-workers are not being held under an authoritative spotlight. This brings us to the conclusion that in the workplace anyone will lie to anyone about anything. This will surprise some of you, but it will be old news to others.

The key piece of information to understand is that there are levels of deceit. Some people can get away with a lie at work because they have support and approval from a group of people who will also benefit from the lie. Some people can get away with a lie at work because there isn't any documentation or individuals that can disprove their story. However, I discovered that the mastery level of deceit at work is from those who are able to get away with a lie because the disregarded rule in question was created by them and broken by them.

The creator of the broken-rule now has the opportunity to enforce this rule by falsely accusing someone that is managed by them, thrown under the bus by them, and eventually fired by them. Now I have seen good acting, but-wow- if someone is able to pull off this type of deceit with policy and laws governed by the company, state, and government......
they surely deserve an Oscar.

I guess you are thinking, *"Well if they have been found out and this is known information, then HR will no longer allow these few deceitful rule makers to get away with it."* Let me put it this way since all HR employees are not like me–some HR professionals also deserve an Oscar for making people think that they always do what is right instead of what is convenient, easy, stress-free, and non-threatening to their own job. Besides, HR employees also have a thing against being in the unemployment line.

pass the whine

pass the whine (Cont'd)

VINEYARD VIEW:

It is not often that an employee will knowingly fall into the trap of carrying out a task that is illegal or immoral. However, in today's economy, employees are feeling more trapped and out of control when the time comes for them to make a decision that will not be viewed as popular by their superiors. It is important to know that employees are still held accountable for their actions even if that action is a direct instruction from an authority figure in the workplace. Therefore, all employees should evaluate their actions to ensure that they are in compliance with the laws of the government, state, and city while following industry regulations. Employees that are being asked to do illegal or non-compliant actions have the option to tell officials within and/or outside of the organization before it ever comes down to the employee's termination due to insubordination.

Fortunately, most corporate officials will rarely insist that you follow through with an action that you have openly declined, due to its illegal or non-compliant nature. Unfortunately, it is more difficult if you are asked to do something at work that is totally legal, but conflicts with your personal views. In order to successfully push-back on these types of undesirable instructions, employees must attempt to communicate an alternative plan that will yield the same results while also supporting their morals and values.

There will be times when this strategy will not work. However, if you find yourself continuously working against your morals and values, you should begin to search for a job that will be a better fit for you. If you are in a work environment that is continuously demonstrating immoral behavior, it is only a matter of time before the conflict of interest weighs gravely on your health and possibly the future success of the company.

Grapes of Wisdom

Each time you are inauthentic, you allow people and situations to continuously chip away at the real you until you no longer recognize yourself.

On Your Mark, Get Ready, Get Set...GO

Now that the employers have overworked a large percentage of their workforce during the recession, many of these individuals are preparing to leave the company for the first opportunity that comes their way. In addition to the overworked, the employees who took a much lower salary (*just to have a paycheck*) are now starting to look for a new higher paying job as well.

Most companies are feeling that they have the upper hand since the economy is proving that there are not many job choices these days. The companies that are opening their doors for hiring are now discovering that they can get more talent for less money or they can just settle for less talent. It is totally understandable for the less qualified individuals to be willing to take a lower salary to have more developmental responsibilities.

The sole purpose of this action is to improve their resume with great job titles and, in some cases, big company name recognition. So they do not think of it as a pay cut. It is thought to be a career investment since pay raises and promotions are hard to come by during a recession. Unfortunately, some companies are still unfairly providing double and triple work assignments to their tenured workforce which has assisted in their company's current level of success.

Some employee's question the whereabouts of company loyalty. I assume we can find it in the same place where employee loyalty is hiding. Back in the day, there were many reasons why people chose to

208

stay with the same employer for a long-term. Those reasons ranged from the excuse of comfort, stocks, retirement, and, most of all, convenience.

Today, it is not expected for an individual to have 20-30 years at one organization. Currently, the average number of years that will make you appear as stable to a job recruiter is three to five years. If you are at a company for 20 years or longer, you are viewed as a soon-to-be retiree or as an individual who has been developed by the same company in a variety of growth opportunities. (*So if your resume does not confirm this growth with multiple titles, you are then looked at as deadweight.*)

I feel as though the workforce should begin to behave like free agents and put the dream of the retirement party and a gold watch to rest. For those of you who are unhappy with your job and are not looking for another, I have what you've been waiting for..... Permission. Don't call another friend complaining about your job, the hours, the money, or your boss. Get your resume updated and just GO!!!!!!!!!!

pass the whine

pass the whine (Cont'd)

VINEYARD VIEW:

In today's workplace, it is viewed as acceptable to have a variety of experience on a resume from different companies. The most important thing that a resume can display is growth. If a resume shows growth to a higher position through internal or external moves, it is looked upon as more impressive than being loyal at one company in the same position. The importance of longevity at a particular organization has transitioned into focusing on the length of experience in a particular specialty/industry.

Although job hopping is still considered a red flag for candidates who seem to switch jobs every 6-12 months, many companies and candidates are on the same page of believing that the 30 year retirement goal is long gone. Therefore, you are encouraged to expand your knowledge, experience, and skill by going to another company when the time is right for you.

Grapes of Wisdom

Aged wine and cheese become finer when left untouched. Most other things that are left untouched will deteriorate-especially brainpower (*or a career path*).

Indecisive Illness

Do you ever feel as though no one at work has the ability or desire to make a decision? I blame the work days that are filled with long meetings, long e-mail chains, drawn out time-lines, and roller coaster discussions on the inability of people to hold themselves accountable for making decisions.

Don't get me wrong, I am clearly aware of the concept of getting buy-in from all the key stake-holders, being a team player, gathering all of the appropriate data ....yatta, yatta, yatta. However, most daily work decisions do not require this long drawn out process. It is as though some employees are afraid to make a mistake. Or worst, they do not want to be viewed as incompetent or non-knowing, so they pass the buck and the responsibility. Well, in my opinion, if you are in a leadership role (*getting paid the big bucks*) and you can never make a decision, then it is quite obvious that you don't know "nothing about nothing".

Everyone wants to pass the decision torch when there is any level of risk associated with a decision, but the same people will fight over the torch and offer to carry it around the globe (*flame burning and all*) when it is time for recognition or reward for the success behind the decision.

If you are fortunate enough to have a degree in your field, years of experience to back up your knowledge, and you are not in the habit of half A_ _ doing things, please do not waste these wonderful traits. The next time you hear someone say, "I think we should check with so and so first," "I think we should run this by you know who," or " I am not sure if this is the right time to move on this," – just know that this is the symptom of a very contagious indecisive disease that is not necessarily a reflection of your lack of competency, but a reflection of that person's fear of owning a decision. So, you should show some true team spirit and provide them with the only known cure for this disease...... look them dead in the eye and say, "Dag, will you stop being so wishy-washy and make a freakin' decision!!!"

pass the whine

pass the whine (Cont'd)

pass the whine (Cont'd)

VINEYARD VIEW:

Unfortunately, some companies blindly set the stage of how comfortable employees feel about making decisions at work. Most Corporate cultures are formed around how bad decisions are handled with the employees who are held accountable. Companies have the options of severely punishing well thought out decisions that turn bad, or they can display encouragement of creativity and learning opportunities by providing constructive feedback and support behind a calculated risk. The act of making a decision is usually not difficult, but taking ownership and being accountable for a decision can paralyze a large number of employees. Companies with fear base cultures will turn the most obvious decisions into a full electoral vote.

Grapes of Wisdom

If you never decide to make a decision, you have decided that your opinion is worthless.

E-mail Hell

W hat did we do before e-mail? How did we communicate in the workplace? How did we make requests of our co-workers? How did we share presentations, project work, and last, but most importantly, how did we CYA?

My friend informed me that she had 800 e-mails in her inbox at work. I think that is un "freaking" believable. It is amazing how e-mail has become overkill in the workplace. People are copying entire distribution lists without taking time to decide who really needs the information. Most e-mail systems have great options that allow us to better manage our e-mail such as files, sorting features, flag notations, and let's not forget the best option... DELETE.

Some important things to remember about e-mails are that they can be legal documents, they never are truly deleted once they reach your company's server, and they can serve as both your friend and enemy. Being behind many investigations at work, I can confirm the importance and respect that should be given to all the e-mails that we compose, send, and save.

If you save an e-mail for CYA purposes, it can be your friend when it's time to slam it on the desk of someone who is on a mission to throw you under the bus. However, an e-mail can be your enemy when you are buried under a heavy workload and you miss a newly created deadline for an important project while you were ignoring the millions of e-mails in your inbox.

Here are some tips to follow to ensure that you avoid the sins of mismanaged e-mails:

1. Categorize your e-mails upon viewing them to quickly read the ones from the people at the top of your priority list.

2. Create files for everyone who is e-mail obsessed and throw all of their e-mails into a file until they ask you about them. If it is important, they will call you after being ignored after some time. Besides, e-mail abusers always send multiple e-mails about the same topic.

3. Flag the important and urgent e-mails that you send to others to prevent your e-mails from being lost in someone else's e-mail hell.

4. Keep a CYA e-mail file to have back-up documentation of all agreements, approvals, or responses from requested information that may not be remembered in the future. If information is not documented, it was not said or done in the mind of someone using selective memory.

OK, this ends my e-mail tips for now. I'm sure that some of you expected me to cover e-mail etiquette. However, I do not totally agree with the amount of training and time that some companies spend on the topic of e-mail etiquette.

Besides, if you receive an e-mail with bold, capital red letters, and multiple exclamation marks, it is not an error and there is no need for e-mail etiquette training. News flash: These co-workers are intentionally YELLING at you, and they are fully aware of their actions!

pass the whine

pass the whine (Cont'd)

pass the whine (Cont'd)

VINEYARD VIEW:

E-mail is a very valuable tool for both the company and the employee when it is used sparingly, professionally, and conscientiously. However, when email is abused and overly utilized, it becomes the workplace's largest obstacle.

Grapes of Wisdom

There's a thin line between abusing technology and allowing technology to enhance life.

You Make Me Sick...

On the way to work, I noticed the number of people on the train that were coughing, sneezing, and blowing their noses. I instantly felt like I was enclosed in a steel tube that was infested with germs that were ready to attack my body at any moment. As I walked into work, I also noticed people who were dragging, speaking with a raspy voice and either popping cough drops or aspirins. Some of my fellow workers proudly announced that they were not feeling well (*As if there is a trophy for the dedicated sick workers who drags themselves into work*).

I would think adults would understand the domino effect of sick people coming into work to spread their germs. They infect healthy people who then get sick who also eventually come into work to infect again the people who thought they were in the clear and somehow managed to regain their health, but got sick yet again due to the germ infested environment that is allowed within the workplace. This can turn into a vicious seasonal cycle that proves to negatively affect productive business activity.

Most companies provide Sick Days to allow employees to stay home and take care of themselves to avoid having entire departments out sick instead of just one team member. However, most employees view their sick days as an opportunity to increase the number of their vacation days by faking illnesses (*HR knows this drill. A sudden illness usually occurs on Monday or Friday*).

So if you are one of these people who are selfish enough to share your germs at work when you know "good and well" that you are not feeling GOOD or WELL, please stay home.

pass the whine

pass the whine (Cont'd)

pass the whine (Cont'd)

VINEYARD VIEW:

Sick days are the most popular way that employees increase their vacation time. Unfortunately, it is difficult to predict when or if you will truly need to utilize sick days in the future because you or an immediate family member becomes ill. Some companies do not separate sick and vacation days. These companies have Paid Time-Off (PTO) to allow the employees to utilize a determined amount of paid time off for vacation, sick, personal and/or floating holidays.

When you are sick and have exhausted all of your sick days, vacation or PTO days, you will need to have days off without pay unless you qualify for a short-term disability. This type of leave is only for a short 6-8 weeks period. However, it will protect your employment with the company similar to long term disability if approved. It is important to know the details of FMLA prior to needing short term or long term leave. FMLA (Family Medical Leave Acts) is an act that protects employees by ensuring that they retain their employment when they or an immediate family member is diagnosed with an illness requiring care beyond the employee's allotted time off.

Although a company must preserve an employee's status during leave time, the company has the right to terminate you for "just cause" on the day you return from leave. Some employees misuse the FMLA's allotted time off to prepare for their next job opportunity. However, the corporation also uses this timeframe to prepare for your departure and your transition out of the organization if they suspect something fishy with your leave (*posted Internet pictures from Hawaii is a good clue that you are not truly sick*). So if you are abusing the system, be sure that you have a plan B because once a company has a clue that you are misusing the system, the goal is to send you a strong message of disapproval by extending an earned or strategically calculated reason for termination.

Grapes of Wisdom

Laws are made to protect, but even a watchdog that is for your protection can turn against you.

Hang On In There...

Broadcasting news companies are currently debating whether the economy is truly picking up or if the government is pulling the smoke and mirror trick. I guess it is a catch 22. If we think the economy is shaky, you will save your money and reduce your spending habits. However, if we decrease our spending, the economy cannot grow.

I guess this is similar to the challenge that corporations are currently facing. They are attempting to save money by reducing their workforce. However, if corporations reduce the workforce too much, they do not have the manpower or brainpower needed to maintain or grow their current business. In addition, they also overwork the remaining individuals who are picking up the slack. It is too bad that overworked employees cannot leverage this new dependency that the company has on them. Unfortunately, the companies know that if you decide to jump ship that there is someone else out there who is willing to do the same amount of work for a much smaller paycheck.

Many companies have turned to consultants and temporary workers to solve this issue of balancing cost savings with workload. These types of arrangements allow the company to get the work done for a determined amount of time without providing costly benefits and without any real commitments. The advantages for a consultant who is fortunate enough not to need benefits are to get overtime pay with high bill rates, skip the torture of performance reviews, and avoid long unpaid working hours. A consultant's hours are also kept reasonably to an average of 40 hours or less over a long term period, since the bill rate would eat a company alive if a consultant would work hours similar to a salaried employee (*50 hours or more if we keep it real*).

I know there are many people who are looking for a job and trying to do what it takes to get a steady paycheck once again. So, perhaps the consultant or temporary project manager is the way to go until something permanent comes along. Now I know some of you Naysayers are saying, "It's too risky; what am I supposed to do in-between consultant gigs?"

My response: Some activity on your resume is better than no activity. Some money in your pocket is better than no money. Most importantly, when you are out of a job, you need to do whatever you need to do to keep hanging on in there.

pass the whine

pass the whine (Cont'd)

pass the whine (Cont'd)

pass the whine (Cont'd)

VINEYARD VIEW:

As a HR professional, I have had the unpleasant opportunity to communicate to employees that their services were no longer needed at an organization. There have been many reactions to this type of news. However, the most common reaction is fear. I truly believe that everyone has value. Therefore, there is a job for most employees that will combine their desire and their current or potential skills. The time in between jobs (*especially if you were blessed with a severance package and unemployment pay)* is a time to discover your next opportunity. Please do not assume that your only job choice is to identify the same responsibilities for a different organization. Life's options are limitless.

Grapes of Wisdom

A traffic jam on life's highway is really a pause to provide time to discover what you truly want.

The Whine Toast

Lastly, I hope these discussions have lifted your spirit and enlightened your heart by providing laughter and comfort in knowing that you are not alone in wanting to improve our workplace environment. Now, you can replace your daily whine and possibly your nightly wine with the ammunition of knowledge and awareness. Remember, every employee has a part in saving the corporate culture. The way you view your workplace will create the workplace that you see.

I pray that you will become aware of your own workplace behavior while becoming courageous enough to address the behaviors of others. Together, we can transform today's corporate world into a more positive environment for generations to come.

Cheers!!!

The Vintage Harvest

Hard work on your part does not necessarily equate to good work in the eyes of the evaluators who have their own expectations of what "good" looks like.

A disregarded request for e-mail exclusion justifies immediate e-mail execution. Take control of your inbox.

Much is expected from those who have gained a great deal, but anything can be expected from those who have gained it unethically.

A job, is a job, is a job. People, projects, and pay may change, but the definition remains the same – "you work, they pay, at first, you stay, until one day, you're on your way."

The acts of jerks and jackasses are not symptoms of a non-controllable disease, but their acts remain voluntary, selective, and are totally based on past responses/consequences from their targets. They will do unto you as you allow them to do.

Avoid groups where you are the greatest contributor, the most knowledgeable, or the most competent. Either you are able to learn or grow from others, or you slowly decline while attempting to teach and grow yourself.

A bad day of being who you are will yield better results than a good day of you attempting to be who you are not.

Stress is a self-induced internal reaction that will follow you wherever you go.

Goals that are truly important to you should create self-motivation that will out-last the motivation from others.

The selective memory of others can easily translate into an opportunity to guess your past actions and responses for their benefit; only evidence from you provides true confirmation.

The true meaning of team is Together Execute Actions Masterfully.

Expectations control the emotional responses to unmet deadlines.

Karma has a sense of humor, so whatever you fake to do may eventually come true.

Be careful of how you use the tongue. Proven to be the strongest muscle in the body, it can pick up or tear down the spirits of an entire audience at the same time.

The calm before the storm may be your last chance to run.

If you can no longer take the heat, first decide how hungry you are before leaving the kitchen.

All secret relationships are temporary since privacy or patience is guaranteed to run out at some point.

The "Truth" may cause brief discomfort, but it will ultimately provide relief. A clever "lie" causes false comfort and creates stress and strain.

Hard work is always rewarded even if the actual award is not always in plain view.

Be clever enough to make good assumptions, but wise enough to think beyond what you can see.

People will assume the task to create a perception of you, but it's your job to manage it.

Be careful to honestly classify what you know, what you may not know, and what you think you know-then proceed with caution.

Valuing the people that work hard for you is like giving the "hand that feeds you" a manicure.

Sometimes the people who "know" are at the mercy of the people who "do not know".

Since everyone knows something about certain things and no one knows everything about all things, there are endless opportunities to teach and to learn.

Change is the result of showing temporary differences in front of others. Transformation is the result of making permanent differences when no one is around. Why change? -TRANSFORM.

Initially, situations will either affect your mind, body, or spirit. But, since all three are connected, each will be affected eventually.

Every action has a consequence. The consequence may be big, small, sooner, later, direct, or indirect, but it will always exist.

You should monitor how others utilize your time as you would if they were utilizing your money.

Silent cries for help will produce invisible assistance.

The volume of your concern determines your priority number on someone else's to-do list.

Verbal agreements are like writing on an "Etch 'n Sketch". The agreement exist until things are shaken up a bit.

The tongue can be the most lethal muscle in the body when the mind and heart are disengaged.

Constantly re-doing bad work and avoiding hard work will only create a tired, over-worked, non-achiever.

Whether they are arranged by you or by others, your priorities are always in a particular order at any given time.

Wasted time, wasted money, or wasted advice is the result of a valuable resource that was managed in a negligent manner.

Win-win situations = C^3: Commitment, Creativity, and Collaboration by all involved parties.

If you do not have any Haters, you are surely doing something wrong; jealousy from others is one confirmation of achievement.

Your first observation of productivity as a new team member will most likely be your clearest perspective prior to having your view tainted with jaded explanations or excuses from existing team members.

A beautiful attractive hire that is not qualified to do the job is like a nicely wrapped box without a gift. Neither is appreciated for long.

Although some eat fish and others eat worms, some spend the day in the air, and some spend the day on a farm; all birds are birds. However, it is not considered fair, reasonable, or sensible to treat every bird nor everyone exactly the same while ignoring current needs and individual situations."

To either guess, assume, or think that you know someone's personal business may all lead you great distances from the truth.

Every now and then, sacrifices should be re-evaluated to prevent you from crossing the line of crazy.

Two heads are better than one, but too many opinions from others may paralyze your progress and create a multi-headed monster.

Each time you are inauthentic, you allow people and situations to continuously chip away at the real you until you no longer recognize yourself.

Aged wine and cheese become finer when left untouched. Most other things that are left untouched will deteriorate-especially brainpower.

If you never decide to make a decision, you have decided that your opinion is worthless.

There's a thin line between abusing technology and allowing technology to enhance life.

Laws are made to protect, but even a watchdog that is for your protection can turn against you.

A traffic jam on life's highway is really a pause to provide time to discover what you truly want.

Armstrong's Dictionary

"Half A_ _"- A clean and tasteful way to say that someone is being lazy, trifling and "Ham Scammy" (This last word is straight out of my mom's dictionary)

Jack Ass: (not my own word) However, it's a dumb animal with no desire to have any sense. Many use it as a curse word, but of course not I.

Hell: (not my own word) I define it as a very undesirable and uncomfortable place. However, if you are not living right, you will find out much more about it than I. See the Holy Bible to learn more.

"Crackernacker Bull"- A form of nonsense in which you cannot crack through to bring forth any common sense due its bull type strength. Something that stops the positive flow of logic.

"Nothing about Nothing"-When someone doesn't know about something, but they are so unaware that they do not know that they continue to speak on the topic anyway.

Haters/Hateraid- (not my own words and both should really be in every dictionary by now)
However, I define Haters as individuals who attempt to block the flow of your blessings. Hateraid represents any negativity that flows out of the mouth of a Hater.

"Hatetologist"-Anyone that is very in tune to Haters and has the skill to stop them in their tracks by managing the Hateraid with positivity.

Copyrights

Kumbaya,My Lord—Kumbaya means come by here .It is a Negro spiritual from the 1930's. Learn more at http://en.wikipedia.org/wiki/Kumbaya

Don't Worry be Happy—It is a song by Bobby McFerrlin. Learn more at http://en.wikipedia.org/wiki/don%27t_Worry,_Be_Happy

You Can't Touch This: I was referring to " U Can't Touch This" which is a hit song in the 90's by MC Hammer. Learn more at http://en.wkipedia.org/wiki/U_Can%27t_Touch_This

Registered Trademarks

Zyrtec- It is a allergy medicine sold by Pfizer. Learn more at www.zrytec.com

Epi-Pen- Emergency injections for the emergency treatment of severe allergic reactions sold by Dey Pharma. learn more at www.epipen.com

Office Depot- Supplier of office products. Learn more at http://en.wikkipedia.org/wiki/Office_Depot

Staples- A large office supply chain store. Learn more at http://en.wikipedia.org/wiki/staples_Inc.

Best Buy- A specialty retailer of consumer electronics. Learn more at http://en.wikipedia.org/wiki/Best_Buy

Oscar- An Academy Award, also know as the Oscar, is an accolade bestowed by the AMPAS to recognize excellence of professionals in the film industry. Learn more at http://en.wikipedia.org/wiki/Academy_award

Etch N' Sketch- The lineographic image drawing sketch board by Ohio Art Company. Learn more at http://en.wikipedia.org/wiki/Etch_A_Sketch

References

FLMA (Family & Medical Act) and Short/ Long Term Leave and other leaves- learn more at:
www.dol.gov/whd/FMLA2007Report/2007finalreport.pdf

WARN ACT (Worker Adjustment and Retraining Notification Act)- learn more at: www.doleta.gov/layoff/warn.efm

Title VII and forms of discrimination- learn more at: www.eeoc.gov/facts/qanda.html

Suggested Reading

I hope that your journey will be improved by this book and perhaps one of the books below.

Go Put Your Strengths to Work
Marcus Buckingham

The Smart Interviewer
Bradford D. Smart

Making Work Work
Julie Morgenstern

Attitude is everything
Keith Harrell

Managing Workplace Negativity
Gary S. Topchik

Tools for Teams
Leigh Thompson, Eileen Aranda, Stephen P. Robbins

Working for You isn't Work For Me
Katherine Crowley and Kathi Elster

Excuses Be Gone
Dr. Wayne W. Dyer

Starting From Scratch
Wes Moss

Feel the Fear & Do it Anyway
Susan Jeffers, PH. D

Holy Bible- (There are various translations and It provides everything that you really need to know.)

About the Author

T. Armstrong Dobson has 20 years of corporate experience with multiple fortune 500 companies. She has had manager and staff positions in engineering, training, sales, human resources, and corporate coaching. The opportunity to view the work environment from various angles has given Armstrong insight that has been sought out by many. Due to a passion for people and her Profession in Human Resources, Armstrong has extended her valuable advice through publications, coaching, and speaking engagements. Armstrong resides in New Jersey with her Husband and son.

Please visit www.somuchwhine.com to contact the author, Armstrong Assets, or to purchase additional books

About the Artist
Matthew Barnes, an aspiring artist, is currently pursuing a Bachelor's Degree in Animation at the University of the Arts in Philadelphia, Pennsylvania. He has experience working nationally and internationally in the fields of animation, film, and illustration.

About the Editor
Pearl Myers Wilson, semi-retired English teacher, is a part time instructor at Acorn State University in Mississippi. She shares her passion for the English language by providing editorial work for various publications throughout the nation from her beautiful town of Port Gibson, MS.